T0077981

Epiphanies, Serendipities & Sacred Spaces

Fly Fishing Reflections

JOHN HERSHEY

authorHOUSE

AuthorHouse™
1663 Liberty Drive
Bloomington, IN 47403
www.authorhouse.com
Phone: 833-262-8899

Published by AuthorHouse 10/25/2021

ISBN: 978-1-6655-4225-8 (sc)
ISBN: 978-1-6655-4226-5 (e)

Print information available on the last page.

This book is printed on acid-free paper.

"If there is magic on this planet, it is contained in water."
Loren Eiseley, *The Immense Journey, 1946*

ભ

Acknowledgements

Anna Ross for taking me floundering
John Lawrie for teaching me to bait a hook
NOLS for outfitting me with a fly rod
Coach Flyfish for supplying my first Garcia
GMR for offering the freedom to fish
The others? You know who you are
Fishing buddies
Esler, Sutton, Lief, Pete B, Powell, Jacob, Alwin, BCB,
Patrick, Jimmy, the Lads, James & Cait, Chris, Doug B,
Vera, Bryan, Mur, Charlie M, Elk, Biggs & Walt
And heartfelt apologies if I've omitted your name

Author Note

This collection does not appear in chronological order. The stories shift back and forth in time. For this reason, I include each story's initial completion date along with edit dates.

CℛℬↃ

Contents

Initial Cast

Perspectives
@95 words
July 2021

These stories aren't about fly fishing. They're about what happened as a result of it. But let me back up, set the scene.

I regularly drove New York Old Route 17 in the late sixties when coppers set speed traps for long haired, pot-carrying collegians traveling between home and their respective schools. Slow down around Liberty; take note when passing through Roscoe. What I also noted about the latter was the diner. I didn't know they called Roscoe *Trout Town U.S.A.* but after eating there, we'd cross the river west of town and I'd notice guys wading the water. I vaguely understood they were fly fishers. I didn't know they were fishing the Junction Pool. The confluence of the Beaverkill and Willowemoc, an iconic piece of water in angling literature. I didn't know about Theodore Gordon or A.E. Hendrickson. I'd never held a rod much less seen a fly. Much of the time I was too stoned to care. I only cared about slipping my hand inside a coed's blouse. Almost a decade would elapse before Coach Flyfish tied a beetle before my eyes. Blame him for my addiction. Life is full of surprises.

Like I never thought I'd live in Minnesota for the better portion of my life; never thought our kids would be born there, that they'd move to New York City but continue to call themselves Minnesotans while criticizing its provincialism. I sure as hell never expected to learn to fly fish or have it occupy my time the way it does. I am grateful. I've fished with flies for trout for over forty years.

I use that phrase deliberately. I don't know enough, or possess the requisite skill, to call myself a fly fisherman. But I know you don't need to

1

know much to love the activity. You don't need exceptional skills to love wading the river. What I present doesn't presume to relate the intricacies of fly fishing. The stories describe a relationship to it. The entries chronicle lessons learned, weaknesses exposed, human truths revealed; pleasant serendipities, senses of place.

Not everything you'll read is true. A *true fishing story* is an oxymoron and I possess an Irish passport. I'm fond of an Irish expression, *Why spoil a good story with the truth?* I like a good story. What's true and what's not? For you to decide.

Most of it is.

If you read, I hope you'll take something positive from what's shared. I'm only trying to give back what I've received. All errors are mine.

JWH

Epiphanies

*"The real truth about fly fishing is it's beautiful in every way, and
when a certain kind of person is confronted with a certain kind of
beauty, they are either saved or ruined for life, or a little of both."*
John Gierach, Another Lousy Day in Paradise, 1996

Integrity: Ropin' 'Em

@1910 words
September 2001/August 2019/April 2021

"Bring yer fly rod," Captain Will drawls. It's daybreak on an already
hot August morning at the Scipio Creek Marina near the mouth of the
Apalachicola River. "I don't fly fish but I bet we can git you into sumpin'.
Rig 'er up."

He nods toward my Cabela's eight-weight, a seventy-nine buck impulse
buy which I acquired years before to cast for Alaska salmonids. I haven't
fished it since, failed to employ it effectively when I did.

I want to use the fly rod but I'm no purist. I'm a small stream, four-
weight trout guy with virtually zero salt water casting experience. If I can
catch fish more readily with spinning gear, so be it. Which is what I say
to Captain Will, a twenty-seven year-old born and reared Apalachicolan.

"Let's hunt up some bait." He pushes away from the dock while I rig
the rod and attach a yellow Clouser to a sturdy tippet.

Will quickly locates a school of pogies in a channel between two small
islands. He throws and hauls a cast net which, when retrieved, pulses
with gleaming four inch minnows, members of the menhaden family. He

deposits the squirming contents into a bucket, repeats the age old process and points the bow toward the Gulf.

Within minutes my guide spots a trio of redfish mudding in the shallows at the edge of the Spartina grass. "Git up 'n cast," he commands. "Quick."

My first attempt falls short; the next veers wide. The reds spook.

"'Specs we might need a bit mo' castin' practice," Will observes without criticism or rancor.

We make the seven mile run to West Pass, a channel dividing Little St. George from St. Vincent, a pair of undeveloped barrier islands. St. Vincent is larger, thick with woodland and game. You can hunt boar or bag a Sambar deer there, just watch out for the salt water crocs. St. Vincent once served as a winter home to the long-vanished Apalachee. Credit Hernando de Soto with their demise. All that remains of their civilization are shards of the pottery they left behind. If you find any, let them be.

Will examines the water. "Tide's wrong. Water's too murky."

Disappointed but undaunted, he steers onto the glassy Gulf and aims for an islet, three miles distant. "Currents might be right out there," he offers.

Barely visible at distance, the sand bar Will calls an island teems with raucous bird life—terns, oystercatchers, gulls, sandpipers—but my guide doesn't like the water. He really doesn't like that there are no other fishing boats in sight. He flicks on the radio and talks Location with his buds.

We decide to return to West Pass and anchor in parallel with a collection of guide boats. The tide pulls our skiff taut against the anchor line. We cast off the stern, our stainless hooks tipped with live bait, and let the minnows do their magic.

The guides talk among themselves, shouting back and forth in familiarly rehearsed and jocular tones. They share success stories, speak of big fish and trade insults thereby entertaining their paying guests. It is obvious they are ignoring one guide who's anchored his red boat east of conversational range.

"Dude dudn't share Intel," Will deadpans when asked. "He dudn't talk to us. We don't talk to 'im."

We sit through twenty action-free minutes before the next boat over lands a catfish, which the guide mercilessly dispatches with a priest. "Trash fish," he drawls, adding a collection of uncomplimentary words about its heritage. It floats away with the tide and gulls take immediate note.

Will is antsy, talks relocation. He moves to the steering column. "Pull the anchor?" he asks as another fisherman nets a handsome speckled trout and displays it for all to see.

"Why don't we hang a little longer?" I suggest.

We have three working rods set in holders and keep an eye on them rather than risk losing one overboard if a fish takes, which is what happens now. The action proves steady, if not spectacular. The trout, ranging from eighteen to twenty-four inches, offer muscled resistance.

I don't count our catch or time the bite, but by conservative estimate in less than two hours we net at least thirty fish and lose another dozen. As I grab one active rod, Will catches my eye. "We ropin' 'em."

"Huh?"

"We ropin' 'em, man. You know, ropin' 'em in." He pulls an imaginary rope, hand over hand, into his waist and grins, truly delighted to be squiring a happy client.

What else comes to the boat? A small hammerhead, a three foot black tip, several ladyfish. We don't keep them but Will happily displays the specs to his comrades before sliding them into a stained white cooler.

He mentions something I don't understand about an *Individual Lifetime Resident License* his dad bought him for a couple of thousand bucks, a type of permit the state of Florida no longer issues.

"Ah can keep seventy-five a day on it," he claims. "You don't mind me keepin' 'em, do ya? Ah got you covered but ah need to keep a passel for the sheriff. Ah owe 'im."

I don't ask why. I don't need to know.

But I won't say I don't wonder *why* Will *owes* the sheriff.

I'm also guessing I've caught my limit and I don't know if fishing with a guide changes that.

I should know but I don't.

What I do know is that of the five boats in the pass the men in the red boat aren't seeing much action. Each time I glance over, their rods sit unattended. The guide glares daggers over the heads of his sullen clients at our jovial group.

When the action slows we cruise back into the bay to search for gulls flocking and diving over roiling bait fish. When we find them I cast the fly line into the churning water and come away with several ladyfish and a catfish. Will treats the latter precisely like his guide friend. "Garbage eater," he chides.

Afterward we're cruising crab pot buoy shadows, hunting for lurking tripletail and hoping for a chance to cast a fly to one, when a voice breaks over the radio. "Cap'n Will, Cap'n Will."

The crackling, disembodied voice belongs to one of the West Pass guides. "Remember those bait shrimp I loaned you? It's payback time, brother. Where are you now? Over."

"S'rimp?" Will's brow knits. He shares an uncomprehending look as he lifts the microphone. "Whatchoo talkin' 'bout? Ah've got a client here hopin' to cast a fly at a tripletail. Call me later. Out."

Will punches off the radio. "Ah never borrowed no s'rimp," he scoffs. He spots a tripletail and maneuvers the boat into casting range.

The fish refuses my fly.

Several minutes later we're talking about ending the day. We're located well west of Apalachicola and there's not a soul fishing nearby. A pair of oystermen work their tongs over their beds under a broiling midday sun. If we're sweating, the oyster guys are really sweating. Then a boat appears on the horizon. It's aimed at us. Someone is coming a long way out of his way to deliver a message.

The guide who wanted Will's shrimp.

The older man cuts his engine and drifts alongside. He wears an exasperated expression and shakes his head. "Son, when I'm talkin' radio nonsense, it means we need to talk." He pauses before adding, "Off the record. Shift channels."

He confides he overheard the ostracized red boat guide report Will to the bay constable for keeping too many trout. An FWC officer is waiting for us at the river entrance. He'll be interested in counting our fish.

Will and the guide debate the interpretation of *the seventy-five keeper license.* Is the individual license good while guiding? Or do outfitter creel limits hold sway?

Neither man definitively knows the answer but, mission accomplished, our informant pushes off and presses his starter. As he pulls away he cuts the throttle and yells, "Will, you owe me, son." He waves, guns the engine and leaves us sloshing in his wake.

"Ah'm gittin' to owe a whole buncha folks these days," Will comments ruefully. He gazes at me while I wonder at the cause and nature of his obligations. "But ah ain't interested in owin' any mo' to anybody else. How 'bout we dump these fellas and take 'er in?"

We unload all but five fish. It hurts to watch them sink like white lead weights into the mud of the shallow bay.

It's a sin and we both know it.

Our return trip feels uneasy. Will's speech pattern sounds strained and he affects a confident tone to gloss his anxiety as we yell over the engine noise, our faces pressed into the wind.

Will relaxes visibly when the constable is not waiting outside the river mouth.. "We clear," he says and we continue motoring up river under the Eastpoint Bridge, passing the town wharf, lined with working boats, modest restaurants, a motel and assorted pleasure craft. As we near the marina entrance a patrol boat emerges from the ramp basin. The officer motions to us and we pull alongside.

"Ah heard Mike reported me for goin' over mah limit," Will blusters, calling the agent by name. "He's just jealous 'cause we were ropin' 'em, havin' fun, and he wasn't doin' jack for his clients. We were holdin' up fish we caught for 'im to see, to piss 'im off. Then we was releasin' 'em over the side of the boat away from 'im. Dude musta thought I was puttin' 'em in mah cooler."

The patrolman repeats Will's explanation, as if trying to believe the story, fixing it in his mind. He offers no argument. "Mind if I check your cooler?"

He counts five trout.

"Nice ones," he remarks. "Good eatin'."

They talk for a few moments about *the seventy-five keeper license* and the agent pulls away and ties up to the dock. He heads for a phone to request official possession interpretation pertaining to Will's license while we proceed to the ramp.

"Ah still wasn't really worried," Will says while deftly filleting the trout. "Even if ah had to go before the judge, my wife works fo' the judge. Ah give 'im trout, too. That asshole guide was just jealous."

The constable approaches the cleaning table. The *seventy-five keeper* is void if you're guiding.

"Welp, now ah know," says Will. "Sure glad we only kept the five. Thanks." He grins an innocent grin and I wonder what hides behind it. I suspect the officer's thoughts echo mine.

Will hands me three bags of fillets. I give two back. "Keep these," I say. "We're leaving town tomorrow so we won't eat them all. Give some to the sheriff," I joke. "You owe him, right?"

My guide confides, "These won't dent that debt but the wife can fry 'em up for supper."

Jeri broils our fillets in lemon, butter, salt and pepper and serves them for breakfast with fried potatoes and iced tea. The meat separates easily under a fork—sweet, tender and tasty. Not one bone to spit out.

I still regret wasting those fish; still see them sliding, heavily inert, over the gunwale into the salt water. I know now I limited out. A fisher with an ounce of integrity would have known that fact before making his first cast.

✳

Maturity: Please God

@2115 words
September 2002/Summer 2019

The final day of the stream trout season matters more than the first. I shy away from the Opening Day crowd. From pancake breakfasts, the bait and hardware slinging, kernel dunking masses; the fly fishing cognoscenti who spent winters around fly shop coffee pots.

This predilection owns historic antecedents dating to a handful of Minnesota walleye openers. Though the outboard experience, spinning rod in hand, is enjoyable, the Leech Lake throngs put me off. I'd rather fish on a quieter day.

In truth, I could locate an unoccupied piece of Opening Day trout water but it is a conscious decision to avoid the crowd and hold out for a more solitary opportunity during the ensuing week. In thirty-five-plus years of trout fishing I have never participated in the Opener.

I cannot make a similar assertion about the last day of the season, a congruent date in the two states I fish most frequently. Though recent enlightened legislation has extended both seasons, I typically circled September 30th on my business calendar, intent on honoring the season by fishing the closing day without the slightest regard for overcrowding.

My father-in-law was born in Ireland. Over numerous dark pints with him I savored the simple beauty of his Irish expressions which painted pictures in my mind. A small bit to eat is *a daisy in a bull's mouth*. Experiencing a gourmet French dining experience is *like feeding biscuits to a bear*.

Through listening, I perceived St. Patrick's profound influence upon the Celtic people. When my father-in-law bade goodbye to a friend, he habitually added *Please God* to the declarative statement.

I puzzled over the phrase for several years, surprised by Jimmy's seemingly selfish attitude. Of asking to live long enough to experience meeting the friend once more.

Now I know different.

Please God is a simple statement of faith, meaning: *I will see you again if it pleases God.*

If it is God's will.

Though the strength and fervor of my faith waxes and mostly wanes, fishing on September 30th bears little relationship to taking a few final casts or catching one more trout. It is a way of giving thanks for the grace granted to fish another season. At sundown on the final day, I habitually light a cheap cigar and smoke it briefly before shredding the remains and offering bits of tobacco leaf to the cardinal compass points, to the earth, the sky, the river and the spirits. Now that I more concretely grasp the relative imminence of my own death, I think *Please God, I hope to fish through another trout year.*

It is not a statement of faith. I am begging.

On drives to the river I typically manufacture a game plan, a predetermined strategy including how far to walk, what pools to fish, what flies to use. Though I seldom adhere to the plan, it does provide a level of comfort for a person who likes to have one.

I resolve on this day—the Saturday *before* closing day—to begin at the Tractor Crossing, a pool which produced regular and sometimes aggressive evening rises during the year. Though unsure of the actual walking distance to the run, it is a haul, a forty-minute hike. I am likely to have the water to myself.

Game plan in place, my mind wanders through a mixture of thoughts, of the irony of the vagaries of my thought patterns while driving to a river whose native appellation means *mixture*, until, for some inexplicable reason I end up considering a passage from John Barth's *The Floating Opera* wherein the protagonist subscribes to the precept of unpredictability before cautioning the reader to avoid unpredictability in all matters, which thereby renders unpredictability predictable.

Maybe you'll appreciate that distinction more after a toke or two.

The notion of *being unpredictable*, of *not* fishing on closing day, takes root. Why not make this evening the final outing of the trout season? I possess all the necessary ingredients. Cool, overcast weather. Time. An uncrowded river. I even have some bad tobacco. Only gradually does the consideration drift away, an idea as shallow-rooted as a maple tree, lost as I park and string up.

It doesn't take long for the game plan to fall apart, about a hundred yards downriver at a meadow where environmentalists deposited mountains of riverside soil and rock, effectively stabilizing a dramatically eroding bank and significantly improving the habitat.

Immediately upstream, trout are rising in a run I've christened *Powell's Elbow*, so named for its shape and for the fact my friend John Powell owned that particular stretch, regularly hoisting trout from its depths. It is there I learned from him the basics of effective nymphing. The configuration of the river and the flow velocity have changed since Powell moved away but I still fish it and think kindly of a former fishing friend. In short order, the game plan is abandoned and I am casting a caddis over feeding trout.

I am a slow and deliberate thinker. Ideas must come right up and bite me in the ass before I catch on. This is true of the moments I spend in Powell's Elbow. My rational mind knows Blue-winged olives hatch on overcast and cool fall days, but I remain blind to their presence, focused solely on the dimpling water. After a few dozen fruitless casts with the caddis, it feels appropriate to change flies. Only then do I consider the water, the surface littered with hundreds of mayflies. Blue-winged olives are hatching.

A #18 immediately catches a trout. And then another and another. And more. Enough to render the day sufficient unto itself. I leave the pool not *needing* to catch another fish but still *wanting* to. And yes, this does indeed seem like a good day to close out the season. I'll take my chances at the Tractor Crossing.

The water there is quiet as I approach but a pair of kayakers is making noise upstream. They're arguing. Something about the *bullshit low water*. They've just dragged their boats over a stony shoal and have resumed paddling as they approach.

"At least you're paddling now," I offer brightly. The news that they have about seven miles to the takeout and that there's a lot of low water between here and there might prove discouraging. I keep my peace.

They are embarrassed I've overheard their bitching. The crabbier guy gives me the finger. The other shrugs an unspoken apology.

The crabby guy's rude gesture makes me wish I'd told them how far they needed to paddle but I am comforted by the knowledge that around the next river bend, a right angle turn where the flow meets the canyon wall, the water widens and shallows significantly as it courses along a beveled limestone cliff moist with moss and crowded with ferns. It is perhaps the longest unbending length of river in the entire canyon. I know it's shabby but I hope they'll have to walk the entire length of the shallow rocky course I call the *Back Stretch.*

I am a curious person and tag surreptitiously along to find out.

There is a run immediately past the bend where the current quickens briefly and then pools up. A postage stamp of sandy beach lines the inside of the curve where a pair of boulders, perched shoulder-to-shoulder like lineman against the far bank, provide excellent cover. I twist the cap off a Leinenkugel, sit on the sand, light a birch tipped Hav-A-Tampa and peer downstream.

The kayakers are pulling their boats, their words unintelligible but the tone unmistakable.

Three trout begin to rise sporadically. Each holds in a distinct location relative to the boulders. I bide my time, finish the beer, stub the cigar and park it behind my ear. The fish are rising more regularly.

I have bollocksed up more than my fair share of casts toward feeding fish, each attempt an act of faith. But this time three casts take the three beautiful trout, the last barely hooked and bright with spawning color. I silently thank him for the privilege of connecting with his absolute wildness. "You beauty," involuntarily pops out of my mouth as I release him.

He angles toward the bottom and is gone. Just like that.

As I consider the next cast, the voice of maturity speaks.

You've fished a lovely hatch and taken three wild trout on three successive casts. It's time to return to the Jeep. Time to call it a season.

A good way to end. And good for me to know when to end it. I relight the tobacco and pass a few quiet moments next to the river, losing myself in jumbled thought, recalling an embarrassing time when I possessed no such wisdom, of a time at dusk in the No Trespassing pool where fish fed voraciously and I couldn't get enough. Avarice owned me. I cast long after I could see well enough to unhook the trout. In my greed and haste I treated them less than kindly because I wanted to catch the next one, too. Sometimes tearing the flesh around their mouths as I yanked the hooks free.

A musician once wrote, "I was so much older then, I'm younger than that now."

I am still surprised when I gaze into the barber's apron and discover, as if for the first time, the proliferation of shorn silver beard in my lap. Now more than halfway home and sufficiently seasoned, I no longer take trout expeditions for granted and remain genuinely grateful for the gifts I have discovered while *fly fishing*.

This is a day to remember: a mixture of images, textures and sounds. The bright blue flash of a kingfisher glinting in a shaft of sun as it banks into a turn. A cloud of midges massing above the Dartmouth Pool. The feel of the current tugging insistently against my waders. The piercing cry of a Cooper's hawk pursuing a sparrow as both vanish into a streamside thicket. The taste of fall in the air. A collection of bright gold maples highlighted against the canyon wall. The stubborn resistance of a trout on my line. The feel of the cold, firm flesh of the last deeply colored trout as it slips out of my hand and swims home.

I finish the cigar and make the customary offering to the directions, elements and spirits. It is a long hike to the truck.

Later I sit at the Copper Kettle where after years of occasional post fishing draughts, I have discovered friendships with some of the barkeeps. I know they serve a mean prime rib sandwich. Wedge a couple of German lagers around the plate and it makes a fine meal.

In this case a blonde college age server places my meal before me. She is beautiful. I should know her name and am embarrassed to admit her shape is more familiar than her face. Shame on me.

When the girl places a second draught on the bar she raps her knuckles on the wood. "Season's almost over? This one's on me."

I raise my stein and thank her. "Here's to maturity," I say. I mean it.

Moments later I take leave and thank the girl once more for the beer. It's as much attention as pretty blondes pay to me these days. I am flattered. "See you next year," she says.

I smile and wave and step outside. "Please God," I announce to the cooling night.

Of course it is easier to walk away from the last cast of the trout season and a free beer knowing I have not actually taken my last cast. In early November my buddy Lief will tell me the steelhead are in. I will drive north to the Brule, dress my line with multiple split shot, work legendary pools with imitation salmon eggs, slip and take an icy bath and cast to fish

I most assuredly will not catch. It's a trip I've taken once each year for the past five with the expectation of taking a skunking.

Last year I fished upstream from the County FF Bridge where steelhead might hold against a gravelly bottom. A younger man approached while carefully evaluating the river.

"Seen any?" he asked from the bank.

"Nah. I'm a rookie."

"Well, you're in a good spot." The Local knows a Downstater when he sees one. He adds, "How long you been comin' up?"

"A couple years."

"Shoot," he said, "you got a ways to go. Took me seven to catch my first."

This is real maturity and it's all good. As long as I'm on the river with a rod in my hand.

Please God.

✻

Advice: The Intel

@935 words

June 2017/February 2019

Powell and I take mental snapshots of the river map in the Driftless Fly Fishing shop. In case we need an alternate plan. We've just heard the local Intel:

"The river's still cloudy but caddis are starting to appear. You might see some sulfurs. We hope so; haven't seen any yet. Hope the recent downpours didn't wash them past Lanesboro into the Mississippi. The river's probably clearer up at Forestville and in the headwaters. If I was fishing, that's where I'd go..." So said the young fly shop guy whose eyes are bright and hard and stony. His wet waders hang from a hook on the shop's front porch.

Not a promising report. Especially since we've driven over a hundred-and-twenty miles to get here on a too-bright-for-good-fishing afternoon.

At least I got to drive Powell's new Silverado. He spent the trip on the phone, planning the menu with the wife and caterer for his younger daughter's high school graduation open house.

Vastly entertaining stuff.

Really.

The substance of human relationships aired on speakerphone. Particularly when the wife's tone occasionally turns caustic. Meant to make Powell feel he shouldn't be fishing with me the day before the party but rather doing his turn as a full time event planner.

Plus I love driving a pickup when I get the chance. A thing I've long wanted but will never own. Powell's truck is equipped with a generous supply of bells and whistles. I felt more like a pilot than a driver. Great fun.

We depart the shop and check the river at the Highway 52 Bridge, the place we always go. The river's clear and sparkling. So we do what most guys do: ignore the advice we requested. We wader up, mount our bikes, pedal down the paved trail, stash our rides in the brush and hike in to the Sheriff's Pool, an old favorite.

The sun glints off the water and the river flows as bright and beautiful as any Montana creek. Redstarts fuss in the riverside thickets, likely nesting nearby; waxwings launch feeding sorties from the tree tops.

This is our first clue. The waxwings are feeding on airborne caddis.

The caddis flies the Driftless Guy said we *might* see. What we think is: the trout *might* take a floating imitation, or perhaps an emerger. The sulfurs *might* come on this evening.

There's always hope. That's what fishermen live for. Fisherwomen, too. The Rise.

We spend a couple of productive hours in the run. The trout take wets and emergers and down-and-across Pheasant Tails, even a couple of Elk hairs on longer casts in moving water. I never get around to working a bugger but I bet it would've worked, too. "The fish are hungry," Powell says. "A good sign."

Shortly after six we plot our next move. We can easily access more distant runs with our bikes but we've seen no one else on the river. There's plenty of water in sight. But there's always new water around the next bend and our conversation goes something like this.

We could bike farther downstream and if nothing happens there we can easily return to the Sheriff's.

But Sheriff's is great water. Why spend valuable time biking when we can be fishing?

Let's stay local. Hike a little ways downstream and check it out.

That way if nothing happens we can easily return to the Sheriff's.

We bushwhack out to the edge of a recently planted field and walk beside a river we hear but can't see. Within five minutes we chance on a sort-of-trail another fisher has broken and, from a perch high above the river, Powell spies working fish. He scoots nimbly down the bank. I locate a more easily negotiable path, a fishing length below Powell, and clamber down. A totally accurate word.

My friend's into a decent fish by the time I start casting. Then another. Sulfurs are beginning to appear. The fish turn on for the next two-plus hours. Powell echoes his former statement. "The fish are totally hungry."

The action proves steady and regular and trout rise and splash up and down the river in response to the increasing proliferation—another totally accurate word—of hatching sulfurs. We're not fish counters by nature but we each catch more than we care to tabulate. But we are fish-measurers. To be fair (and conservative), we each catch a few in excess of fourteen inches. Good fish by our standards.

Somewhere in the midst of casting and catching, I wonder aloud about the Driftless Fly Fishing Intel. Surely, we reason, the sulfurs hadn't come on for the first time this evening. The hatch is robust. The kid minding the shop was clearly a fisherman. He had The Look in his eyes; he'd hung his waders to dry in the sun outside the store so he'd been out. He must've been clued in to the river. Why did he point us toward the headwaters?

To deliberately mislead us? Direct a couple of Twin Cities rubes away from a good local spot?

But, if he meant to mislead us, why don't we see any other local fishers on a beautiful Friday evening during prime trout season?

"Maybe we're too far from the road for most guys," Powell ventures.

We don't spend much time pursuing this line of questioning. The trout are biting and we fish until the action grinds down. Then we hike and bike out in the twilight and crack cold bottles of Rogue ale at the truck.

I think *epic* is a word Powell *might* use in describing our experience.

I am.

✳

Responsibility: I Should Know Better

@1205 words
October 2007/Summer 2019/April 2021

I am floating in a canoe on a northeast Minnesota lake, connected to a stocky rainbow whose thrashing has attracted the interest of a mature female raptor. The eagle swoops, her dark plumage shining purple, one yellow atavistic eye gleaming with predatory intent. Shifting the fly rod to my left hand, I firmly check the line, grab a paddle with my right and helicopter it above my head while responding to avian primal screams with my own profanities.

The bird's discretion subdues her greed. She voices a final contemptuous and quarrelsome note and returns to her post atop a spindly and expiring white pine.

"Shame on you," I chide. "Catch your own fish."

Unbelievably, the rod continues to vibrate against the trout's resistance and the reel helps me bring the fish to the gunwale.

Beautiful.

Then, a mere inches from capture, the largest trout I've ever hooked slips free from my grasp and melts into the black depths.

"Shoulda had a net," I confide to the eagle.

There and then I vow to spring for a landing net.

◈

Back home, the electronic world presented a daunting variety of options. Handcrafted beauties, lightweight four-ply cocobolo plantation wood numbers, going for a hundred-and-fifty bucks. Even the standard cherry wood models fitted with durable French clips felt dear.

My resolve quickly lost steam.

In the end, I rationalized my frugality. I'm a No Gadget Kind of Guy. My vest is more than twenty years old. It contains one modestly appointed fly box, a spare collection of tools, floatant, split shot and tippets, the outfitting based on a reductionist philosophy of keeping it simple and buying new stuff when the old stuff breaks. Or when I lose it. I'm not a

---

JOHN HERSHEY

Mennonite for nothing. So I stowed away my Visa and relegated a landing net to the category of Extraneous and Unnecessary Equipment.

◈

Then on an eastern swing with family in tow, A Good Deal presented itself when least expected, at the now-defunct Little Store in a quiet Catskill village, where fly fishing purists honor the memories of Theodore Gordon, George Labranche, Edward Hewitt, A.E. Hendrickson, Winnie and Walt Dette and Sparse Grey Hackle.

The Little Store sticks in memory as my kind of place. An old fashioned hardware emporium catering to a variety of camping, home repair and upkeep needs, including an affordable and wide selection of trout flies and more specialized angling gear. A shop where our pair of waist-high boys created minor havoc in the narrow aisles and no one paid much mind. You could get what you needed and what you didn't at the Little Store. And for a better price. Count it a bonus no one would cast a disparaging eye if you bought a Mepps instead of a fly.

An aluminum frame landing net for fourteen-ninety-five appealed, as did a Little Store tee bearing the inscription *Trout Town USA*. Not long after, I toted the new net to my home water and endured a skunking, an outcome that no longer insulted since I owned enough years to understand that *the process and the experience* matter.

Sometimes *the process* is *the experience*.

Sometimes you catch a big trout.

Nevertheless I felt compelled to rationalize the shutout. Had I offended the fishing gods by carrying a landing net? Had I acted presumptuously, cavalierly assuming I'd experience the grace of catching a trout and subsequently netting it?

The rational side of my mind understood that my empty creel accurately reflected a personal lack of angling expertise, but it felt best to avoid disquieting the spirits. I suspended the net by its rim from a nail at the inside of the northern apex of our garage roof. It hangs there still, now antiquated, the netting no longer in vogue with the advent of softer, kinder fabrics.

Despite the obvious and essential fundamental function of a landing net, I refused to carry one. I pinched my hook barbs and handled my own fish as gently as possible. Most of which proved to be, admittedly, small and easy to manage. So what if a few got away?

◆

Several years later, I made a budget-conscious solo trip to the Bighorn, rented an amenity-free room and passed four blissful days probing the riffles and runs of a gorgeous, golden-banked western river. Fish came to hand every day. Not a lot, but enough. Even the larger ones swam free from captivity with minimal negative piscatorial impact.

Or so I believed.

On that changeable equinox Saturday I made an improbably long, Hail Mary cast to a rising fish. To my surprise and delight it immediately slurped a #18 Adams. After a strenuous and lengthy reel-zinging adventure, I dragged the beautiful creature unceremoniously ashore. A twenty-two inch rainbow. Giving silent thanks to unnamed spirits I revived her and sent her on her way.

A half an hour after release I discovered the trout drifting lifelessly along the bottom of the river.

I felt like a murderer.

Guilty as charged. Fishing irresponsibly without proper equipment.

Shame on me. I should know better. Especially at my age.

I reeled in and stopped fishing. The mental image of the expired trout haunted my evening reading and drinking and morphed into a bourboned haze.

The next morning I inspected the picked-over, end of season inventory of a Fort Smith tackle shop and considered the cost of the pricey, multi-layered hardwood landing nets before settling on the cheapest one, a twenty-five dollar special with a black aluminum frame. As an afterthought, I laid out an additional tenner for a sturdy keeper magnet. Feeling sufficiently contrite, I drove to the 'Horn for a final day on the river.

A Pheasant Tail drifted through skinny, fast-moving water proved an effective strategy and I happily hooked, netted and released a series of brown and rainbow trout as the makings of a smile crossed my face. Apparently my spiritual angling balance had been restored. I moved to a new spot with the tacit assumption that gentle minded Kismet accompanied me on an autumn day that felt better than the weather boded.

Then my six-weight Orvis Clearwater snapped near its base on the very next cast, irrevocably broken, the shattered graphite tool reduced to a lifeless stick. Dead rod in hand, I eyed a fleet of dark bellied stratus slumping across the heavens and recalled a few lines from one of the Bard's sonnets, a reference to "the basest clouds" riding "with ugly rack" on the sun's "celestial face," then "stealing unseen to west with this disgrace."

Indeed, I had been disgraced. Judged and found wanting by the fishing deities delivering their implacable edict, reinforcing the immutability of karmic redemption, the retribution for fishing irresponsibly now justly meted out. I should have started carrying a net years ago.

It's not about vanity or simplicity.

It's about respecting all living creatures.

I should know better.

Though my trophy trout lost its life, it is my hope the noble fish sacrificed it so her sisters and brothers might survive. At this very moment that landing net rests in the bottom of my fishing duffle, ready for use. And the image of that dead trout drifting whitely along the river bottom continues to haunt my memory.

N.B. Midwest Fly Fishing magazine publisher Tom Helgeson included a version of this story (Questions of Responsibility) in the October 2009 edition. I knew Tom through work connections and we shared conversation and coffee in his office several times so, on a whim, I sent him the story. I didn't mean for him to publish it. I never thought he would. Though Tom did not send any remuneration in return for using the piece, I never expected any. The byline acknowledgement identifying me as a "freelance writer and novelist who lives in St. Paul, Minn." felt sufficient. In early 2010, Tom and I drank coffee together for a final time when, sadly, he told me of his battle with cancer. He wrote a check for a hundred-and-fifty dollars for the story. I think it was his way of saying goodbye to a friend and settling his accounts. You can read more about Tom in the notation at the end of A Surfeit of Rods which appears in this anthology.

I also confess that the net lesson didn't exactly stick. I've stopped carrying one on local trips where the trout are manageable. And on a recent cold November day I fished the Whitewater with Pete B. Much to my surprise I hooked a radiant fifteen inch rainbow and needed to ask Pete to net it. Pete B always carries a net.

✷

Generation Gap: Urban Fly Fishing

@1860 words
June 2002/March 2019

I am fishing an urban river, float tubing in the Mississippi Gorge, awkwardly casting a big surface fly for smallmouth. Two hundred feet above, the Franklin Avenue Bridge bustles with city traffic. Upstream, the Minneapolis skyline looms over the canyon. Hardly the pastoral setting associated with fly fishing. Yet, as near as the city appears, I feel separated from its humming pace. The gorge is deep. The city is Up There. Downstream, the river bends out of view. Its tree lined banks and flood plain have a timeless look. When the Anson Northrup riverboat ferries tourists up from its Saint Paul dock, it's not difficult to time travel. It wouldn't surprise me to find Mr. Twain at the pilot's wheel.

I'm floating in a turnout, a place where the river elbowed a shallow indentation against the east bank and I can comfortably maintain casting position out of the current's flow. All I really need to mind is the tug and barge wakes.

I must be an odd sight. At least the riverbank strollers who stop and gawk seem to think so. Some point. Some ask about the fishing. One man even talks business. We chat across the distance of some sixty feet and our voices echo under the concrete span.

"I've got some casting to do and the light is failing," I offer.

The speaker hesitates for a moment. "Oh...yeah...I get it." He completes the thought. "Talk to you later. I'll call. Bye." He waves and ambles off.

This isn't my first experience fishing with flies for bass in this spot and I sort of know what I'm doing. That wasn't always the case. I've come here a few times now. It all began when I started hardware fishing with Sutton.

Sutton and I met as preschool bachelors, fathers awaiting our children's noontime dismissal, standing among a group of chatty mothers outside the red door of the Jean Lyle School. United by gender we spoke Guy Talk. It wasn't hard. Sutton loves college basketball and holds an especial fondness for the Duke team. I coached women's college hoops for a living at the time and this opened a range of basketball topics for mutual consideration.

We also agreed we fished and, as we later discovered, loved to talk about it. But we spoke different dialects. I talked trout flies; Sutton named bass lures. He once admitted he thought I wore tweed and cast a bamboo rod.

Eventually our kids outgrew preschool. Though they subsequently attended the same parochial one, Sutton and I stopped meeting by the red door. We didn't talk on a regular basis. Sometimes we met after church but basketball remained the coinage for conversation. I didn't know he owned a boat.

A couple years later our wives joined the school board and somehow a post-meeting conversation drifted to husbands. Erin said Sutton fished a lot, he was always on the river. She wondered if I'd like to go with.

Jeri didn't know a plug from a fly. Still doesn't. She probably said something like, "My husband loves to fish and he loves going out in boats."

Erin said she'd tell her husband and Jeri told me the story when she got home.

The phone rang on a sunny Sunday the following fall. "Hey," said a disembodied voice.

"Hey yourself." *Who is this?*

"What are you doing today?"

Who the hell is this? "Hanging out."

"Wanna go fishing?"

I finally know. Sutton. "Yeah. When?"

"Now. I'm heading out to Pool One."

"I don't have the right stuff to fish the river."

"I got you covered. Come over in ten minutes?"

"See you." I hung up and got ready to fish.

We rendezvoused, got Cokes, launched at Hidden Falls and navigated the lock at the Ford Bridge. In less than an hour we were tossing crank baits to the rubble along the left-descending bank near the base of St. Anthony Falls, immediately below River Mile 854. Commercial navigation on the Mississippi begins about a mile upriver from our location. From where we're anchored it is 854 river miles to the Big River's confluence with the Ohio.

Sutton's a science teacher. He explained the fishing regs, the year-round season, lock placement and construction, the history of wing dams, the effect of levying, the draining of backwaters so vital to healthy habitat. I learned about deep-diving and shallow-running Rapalas and how to fish tube jigs. All this and more while spending an enjoyable afternoon with a self-schooled student of the river. We caught bass, a big carp, catfish, some northerns and a sheepshead. I couldn't have had a finer time—and, I'm not lying, we had all the equipment we needed. Boxes and bags of it.

When the sun dipped below the top of the gorge, we returned to the ramp. Sutton winterized the boat, arranged for its storage and the river turned to ice. We met occasionally after church and talked basketball.

Next summer more frequent, but always spur of the moment, invitations ensued. Sometimes Sutton called on his way to the river. Other times he stopped by. Mostly I went with. I think that impressed him: that my marital and parenting agreement flexed sufficiently for unplanned fishing trips. Whatever the case, it pleased me to go almost as often as Sutton asked. I'm like Kenneth Grahame's Water Rat in *The Wind in the Willows*.

"Believe me, my young friend," Ratty says to the Mole, "there is nothing—absolutely nothing—half so much worth doing as messing about in boats."

◈

I am a slow thinker. It takes time for a new idea to sneak up behind me and crack me over the head. It never really occurred to me to take my fly rod when I fished with Sutton, an adventure I shortsightedly compartmentalized as a Hardware Trip. Besides, I was interested in learning a new way to fish. You can cover water efficiently with a spinning rod. And I caught fish that way. Reason enough right there to leave the fly rod behind.

So one afternoon late last summer we floated in shallow water over a rock garden under the Franklin Avenue Bridge, prime bass habitat. I noticed wadeable places well off the bank. I noted the slack current and thought how I could float it in a tube. On the east bank I noticed sections of wooden steps, which traced a jagged line from the river to street level. I thought those thoughts for a while but came to no specific conclusion.

I'd spent a particularly difficult and hot August Sunday, starting with my always reluctant Mass attendance and continuing with a litany of home care chores to which I paid half-hearted attention. Life in America bogged me down. I wrestled with the notion of fishing the Kinni and considered the evening rise, *if* it would happen at all. We'd experienced a topsy-turvy fishing year. A late thaw and heavy runoff ruined most of the trout season. I wavered. Was it worth a seventy mile round trip to find out if a few fish would rise? Or should I crack a couple cold ones and hang out on the porch?

And then the light bulb went on. I could float fish for bass under the Franklin Avenue Bridge.

It takes a few moments to assemble a passable selection of bass flies from an assortment L.L. Bean included as a bonus to some purchase I made over a decade ago. Hairy, gaudy things I can't name. Is one a Dahlberg Diver?

Twenty minutes later I lug a float tube down the river gorge steps, dressed in waders and armed with a rigged fly rod. I enter the Big River cautiously and discover I can float in place with relative ease. I cast in and among the rocks, jerking a deer hair surface lure hoping to trick a bass.

The first is a hefty fellow. The second is bigger. He boils under the fly, misses it, reboils and savagely strikes the fly. He puts a pleasant arc in my six-weight. Maybe fourteen inches of bass? This is fun.

Later I cross over the Franklin span and take a slight detour to put the finishing touches on a successful fishing venture. A pint at Molly Quinn's, an Irish pub owned by a loquacious and long-winded writer who loves his drink. He's a Scot and he owns an Irish pub. I like to think he's seen the light. I'm a Scot with an Irish wife.

Patrons are grouped conspiratorially, heads leaning toward one another, when I enter. The Writer stands in a corner of the bar and bellows out a question for all to hear.

"James Mason," I answer as I take a seat at the bar.

The actor with the male lead in Stanley Kubrick's 1962 version of *Lolita*. Stuff guys my age know.

The group immediately to my left glares at me. "Don't give away the answers," one crabs irritably. He shakes his head disdainfully. The group to my right is a younger assemblage and one of its members writes *James Mason* on a sheet of paper and makes no comment.

"Oh...I get it," I apologize. "It's Trivia Night. I'm sorry." I sip at the Guinness the barkeep sets in front of me and mind my tongue.

Several questions and one pint later the Writer asks about Natty Bumppo and how he is otherwise known. The younger group is stumped. I can't help but overhear their chatter. I nudge a young woman next to me. She has short red hair and her nose is pierced. She's doing her best to look unattractive but she's not. And she's got a nice figure. She's anywhere between twenty and thirty-five but those distinctions blur on me now.

"Think Fenimore Cooper," I prompt.

She shares a blank stare.

"You know, James Fenimore Cooper? The nineteenth century writer? Basic American Lit?"

"Huh?"

"Think *The Leatherstocking Tales? The Pathfinder? The Deerslayer? The Pioneers?*

Still blank.

"*The Last of the Mohicans?*"

"Oh..." She's thinking. "The movie with the cute guy. Daniel Day Lewis?"

"That, too," I allow.

"Hawkeye," the girl concludes. "Hey..." She smiles at me and it brightens my day. "Thanks."

I'm confident my new friend is far more comfortable with the various platforms of current electronic communication. I don't know a GIF from a

Meme, Instagram from Pinterest; never seen an episode of *Seinfeld*, *Friends* or *The Simpsons*. On the other hand, I do wonder how contemporary education has reduced an American Lit icon to comparison with a handsome male actor.

I let that thought slide and sip the last of my Guinness. It's a good thing I don't have to fret about impressing chicks at bars anymore. I was never good at it to begin with. Better to have a wife who loves me and encourages me to fish as often as possible.

On the way home, I cross the river on the Lake Street Bridge and steal a wistful glance at the piece of water I'd fished—the river now an ebony ribbon reflecting city light. I arrive home in five minutes, recline in a porch rocker and savor the cooling city air.

N.B. I never received advisement nor remuneration when a version of this story appeared in the 2009 Winter/Spring edition of The Drake. A casual friend casually advised me of its publication the following August. The current editor apologized for the oversight saying, "They ran a loose ship before I arrived." A polite young staff woman agreed to extend me a lifetime gratis subscription. That's enough. Franklin Avenue Bridge construction has delayed my return to that rock garden in the Mississippi River. There must be other ones.

✴

Age: Too Old to Be This Stupid

@1065 words
December 2014/Winter 2019

The road ascends the bench north of Antelope Flats Road, tracing an ancient river course. I gain elevation and peer into the Snake valley where I note a collection of vehicles parked in a dirt access lot.

Fishermen, I think. *Probably a good place to check out.*

It's beautiful in fact, framed by *Les Trois Tetons*, part of the youngest of the Rocky Mountain ranges aligned neatly along a fault line, razors against the sky.

The following day I steer down the rutted landing road and park among a collection of vehicles. The air is sharp, scented with sage and fall. I string up, don waders and follow a beaten path toward the river.

It doesn't take a genius to realize I didn't park among fishermen. Photographers have set up tripods mounted with cameras and bazooka-like lenses. Most use the meadow ponds as reflecting pools to capture the mountain splendor to the west. Others focus on the wetland, waiting patiently for an elk or moose to appear. It's a sky-blue day and I pause long enough to snap a few handheld images with a Canon Power Shot. Much later a friend will remark about the artistic way I captured the light.

I'm no artist.

The path narrows as I hike through a beautiful marsh edged on three sides by forest. In a matter of moments, I'm entirely alone. Then the path ends at a creek crossing. This is when I start singing. My heart races.

I shoulda brought the bear spray.

I ford the creek and enter the forest, walking in a direction where I know I'll find the Snake, but it's farther than I estimated from yesterday's vantage on the bench. I'm definitely paying attention to where I'm going. I want to remember the way back.

I shoulda brought my GPS.

It strikes me I'm approaching this fishing adventure with a Midwestern mind. This is the West. Everything is bigger. And, potentially, more dangerous. I start to feel more than a little nervous.

I've told no one where I'm going or when I plan to return.

There is elk sign everywhere and I note a rotted fallen tree raked with claws much larger than a raccoon's.

I felt uneasy before.

Now I'm spooked.

I can hear my heartbeat.

I stop and take a few deep and calming breaths while considering my options. I am sixty-five and a stubborn man. I don't want to admit defeat. I want to fish the river. It's a matter of pride.

I need to fish the river.

My emotional discomfort transforms this walk into an Odyssey but I finally clear the forest, carefully noting my exit point. I want to reenter at the same spot on the return hike.

Finally, I spot the river. To reach it I cross a rocky, debris-littered flood plain, its stunted vegetation a bright October yellow. I stand on a steep cut bank, ten feet above the water, and stare into a deep, clear, fast moving pool.

The river is much bigger and faster and wider than I thought.

Upstream the river bends. There's a beach there and the current widens and slows and drops into a fishy-looking riffle. I am distinctly aware I'm totally alone. I remember once more I've told no one where I'm going.

As I approach the beach I wade delicately on the slippery river rock. The footing is treacherous. Especially since I'm not wearing wading cleats.

I realized the same thing the week before when I fished the Madison. That's when I bought an eighty dollar Simms wading staff. The one I left today in the Subaru's trunk.

I say aloud, "I'm too old be this stupid."

Then I stupidly tie on a streamer and wade in. I'm here. I may as well fish.

I cast a sculpin, let it sink and strip it down and across, methodically covering the water. I feel several strikes and then the electric jolt of a solid take. The reel whirs. The rod arcs beautifully. As I struggle to land a sizeable cutthroat I realize I own a Midwesterner's net.

I need a bigger one.

I finally scoop the trout whose tail trails over the net rim.

I never tire of seeing a trout's vivid coloration when it emerges from the deep and comes to hand. I think a silent prayer of thanks and release the fish, then straighten and raise my arms skyward. It is a beautiful day to be on the river, to be alone and sixty-five, to have neglected to tell my friends where I'm going, to have forgotten the bear spray, the GPS, the wading staff and to need a bigger net.

I'm stupid, but I caught a lovely trout.

The fish are kind and I linger for more than an hour before I submit to my unease and head back, not exactly entering the woods where I exited and not exactly retracing my steps but confident of basically heading toward the parking lot by keeping the Tetons at my back.

"No bears. No bears," I repeat as a regular mantra while I hike. I feel deeply relieved when I find the place where I crossed the first creek. I start singing when I enter the meadow. An old Beatles tune.

"I should have known better with a girl like you."

I pass more photographers and find a lost fly rod tip. I think, *I hope the guy who lost this went fishing with a friend.* But that's as close as I come to seeing another fisherman.

I spend the rest of the day on the Gros Ventre, a gorgeous, bony river with friendlier access. Nevertheless, as I wander upriver, wishing for my wading staff that I once again forgot to bring along, there are times when I start singing. I catch cutthroats there, too.

In the evening, I consult Google Earth and realize the truth.

What felt like a very long trek to the Snake was about a three-quarter mile walk.

I've hiked much farther than that to fish in the Midwest. Just not in places where I should have brought bear spray, a GPS, a wading staff and a bigger net.

My Teton Village friend asks about the day's fishing. I pause before admitting the truth. "I probably fished a couple of places I shouldn't have gone by myself. I'm too old to be this stupid."

✳

Entitlement: A Gringo Like Me

@1610 words
October 2016/Winter 2019

"I came to Fort Smith," a grizzled ghillie confided, "because it's at the end of the fucking road."

It wasn't always. Fort C.F. Smith was established along the Bozeman Trail in 1866 during Red Cloud's War when some knew the area as *Powder River Country* while others called it the *Montana Territory*.

Now it is the end of the road. Montana Highway 313 literally dead-ends in Fort Smith at the base of the enormous Yellowtail Dam. The road provides access to the Bighorn Canyon National Recreation Area and a trout rich tailwater fishery.

Ironically named for the chief who opposed the dam's construction, workers completed the project in the mid-1960s. The towering concrete edifice backed up the Bighorn River, flooding an enormous canyon and burying sacred tribal sites by creating a reservoir more than seventy miles long. So long it backs into Wyoming. So desolate the lake and the dam are the only obvious landmarks when flying over it.

Erected to generate electric power, to promote agriculture and control flooding, the dam also birthed a recreational industry. The cold water emerging from its base produces an ideal bug and trout habitat. Hatches can be impressive. The fish are healthy and strong. It is a trout fisher's Mecca.

No one comes to Fort Smith for the scenery or the amenities. A visitor must possess a certain aesthetic to appreciate the sere, sparse high plains. The country possesses no dramatic features like the jagged, snow covered peaks or forested river valleys which decorate Montana post cards.

If you like open country, you'll find it here. If you favor a certain degree of the lack of human-generated sound, you can find the quiet you crave. If you're a barista don't come looking for work. You won't find a latté or, for that matter, a decent restaurant, a drive-through taco stand or a shopping mall. And bring your own booze. The town is dry. Fort Smith's on the Crow Reservation, part of which our government reclaimed in order to build a dam.

What can you find? A motley collection of mobile homes and utilitarian houses, their parking areas cluttered with trailered boats and assorted motorized vehicles, some in running order. There's a church and post office. Inside the one convenience store you'll discover prepackaged items and a casino; outside you can fill your tank at the pump and pay through the nose. The only gas in town. The only gas for miles.

The 2010 census lists one hundred-sixty-one residents. The majority likely caters to the fishing crowd. If they hold jobs located elsewhere, it's a long commute on lightly trafficked roads.

Three fly shops sit within spitting distance of one another on a dusty main street. They sell plenty of flies and all manner of gear. A guide with a drift boat goes for about four-fifty bucks per.

Visiting fishermen rent camp sites, tiny rooms, trailers, cabins. Even a few houses. In the absence of restaurant service, they cook their own food or reserve table settings for chef's choice meals served in dining halls at predetermined times. The well-to-do can satisfy their desires, too. Forrester's resort caters to upscale folks by providing posher cabins and gourmet dining to supplement the first-class trout fishing or cast and blast expeditions.

It's guys like me who come to Fort Smith. Mostly privileged white guys. Guys who think the town's so ugly it's beautiful. The only thing you can do is fish. And drink at night. What's not to like?

And, if you listen carefully, you'll discover we're all good liars. We like a good fishing story. Why spoil a good story with the truth?

This morning more than thirty trucks trailering drift boats queue in front of the fly shops, all waiting for clients. It's September 22nd, the supposed *shoulder* of the trout season. The morning aggregate of guides gives me pause.

What's it like here on a July morning?

I haven't engaged a guide and am here on the cheap, renting a tiny room for less than seventy-five a night, purchasing a sit-down meal plan—breakfast and supper—for convenience sake. The plan is to wade-fish the big river, to wade and cast among the plebeians and cheapskates.

This morning a garrulous wadered man of my approximate vintage approaches me in the Three Mile access lot. "Bighorn's not like it used to be," he volunteers.

Nothing is, I think.

"I fished the Bighorn in eighty-one when it opened. We parked here." He motions to the maintained gravel lot, "It was a rutted pasture. We caught fish as long as your leg. Not like now."

He launches into a diatribe about the crowded river, the flotillas of drift boats and the reduced fish size. I quietly wonder why the hell he's here if the fishing sucks so bad.

He's right though. I've been coming here off and on—and typically during the autumnal equinox—for more than twenty years. Things have changed.

A guide's fee now exceeds the limits of my emotional capacity to pay for a float trip. The only place to buy an *á la carte* meal is shuttered now. Polly's. A restaurant of questionable standards run by stoners. You could bring your own beer.

The most regrettable change is the arrival of Wi-Fi and cell service. I so reveled in getting beyond contact range and continue to rue the fact that people value electronic connection more than human interaction.

Last night at supper I sat solo in the Bighorn Angler dining hall as fellows crowded at tables with their companions. A pair of gray-haired ministerial types occupied a two-top in my direct line of sight and said grace before dining. Thereafter, one spent most of his time, even while eating, with his nose buried in his cell.

You know the opening chapter of *Moby Dick*? The part where Ishmael determines when it's time to go to sea? It's when he feels the press of civilization and is forced to resist the urge to step into the street to knock men's hats off.

That's how I felt.

I wanted to knock off the cell reverend's hat. I didn't. But I regret not inviting the other pastor to dine with me.

So yes, things have changed on the Bighorn and in Fort Smith but I am not disposed to add fuel to my complaining friend's rant. I allow him space to complete his train of thought and listen politely as he describes his fishing prowess. We part on agreeable terms, leaving me completely at ease with the idea that I still love fishing the Bighorn River.

I have fished with flies for trout for forty years. Though I should reasonably anticipate some measure of success given my time on the water, I am always surprised and pleased to come west and catch trout on my own in a big river. I don't think I'll ever tire of guiding a strong, brightly colored rainbow into my net. I hope not. I no longer *need* to catch fish. But I still love to.

On this trip I spend the better parts of four days exploring the Bighorn *à pied*. The weather is autumn-perfect for the non-fisher—blue skies, wispy clouds, mild temperatures and minimal wind. I encounter a modest rise to one patchy spinner fall, locate a few holes where fish are willing to grab nymphs and catch numbers sufficient to each day.

On three successive evenings I drive up a road that corkscrews into the Bighorn foothills to the *Ok-A-Beh* Marina, an access point for reservoir boaters. After five approximate miles and elevation gain, I arrive at a turnout where log rail fencing encloses a modest exhibit celebrating the Crow culture.

I brake, kill the engine and step out to enjoy a spectacular view of the largely undeveloped and unoccupied northern plains. A collection of wrinkled buttes and hills extends like bony fingers to the northeast. Dramatically staged sedimentary cliffs line a distant creek. The silence is sobering and sacred, broken by natural sound.

A crow caws.

The wind voices its presence.

Coyotes yap.

As the sun sinks below the horizon, the spirits of the ancients emerge to roam the land.

Imagine the country in a former time, before invading Europeans stole it, a practice tribes of all stripes and hues have done from the beginning of human existence. Try to imagine the land before white men arrived with powder and muskets and traps and rifled barrels and whiskey; before the land surrendered to the plow, to seed and to barbed wire and livestock; before steel rails and concrete paths spanned it.

On my last morning I stop into the Yellowtail Market to buy a Coke for the road. The store is sparsely stocked; some shelves stand empty. A side door beckons gamblers to try their luck at the slots. The depressing venue is a monument to The Have Nots who reside in a place patronized by The Haves.

A middle aged Crow woman, eyes averted, her figure as broad as tall, mahogany skin smooth except for the wrinkles by her eyes, mutely accepts my payment. She has no interest in conversation. I'm just another gringo.

In that moment I feel a profound sense of entitlement, like a trespasser on her property.

I'm sixty-seven, likely making the rounds of western fishing holes for the final time. Though I love fishing the Bighorn River and visiting warty Fort Smith, my encounter with the clerk gives me pause.

I may never visit Fort C.F. Smith again.

Sure, the fish are bright and buxom. But the land? It doesn't really belong to us rich white folks. If you go, tread lightly there.

N.B. I intended to write this piece as a kind of "Come to Fort Smith" essay but it wound up going sideways. Then on the day I rewrote it for inclusion here I accidentally ran a Bighorn Angler fly shop ball cap through the washer and dryer. It emerged clean—but a shadow of its former self, its sizing reduced to a limp noodle. If I wear it now I will most certainly look like the old fart I have become and I don't need any more help on that score. I'm taking it as an omen. I may never fish at Fort Smith again. Then again, I might want to buy a new hat.

✳

Faith: Thinking About God

@1455 words
September 2002/Winter 2019

I don't like going to church. I never have. I can't remember one instance when I eagerly anticipated a Sabbath service or came away from one feeling anything more than a quiet sense of relief.

I have nothing against God, the Creator, and marginally adhere to a broadly defined and inclusive Christian belief system. On one point I keep certainty. I sure don't find the Lord in church. Given absolute freedom of choice, I'd attend rarely. Funerals, weddings and baptisms suffice.

My scars, innocently inflicted, run deep. I was reared on the campus of a nonsectarian Christian boarding school for boys where my father taught and where its founder and headmaster baptized me on Easter afternoon, 1951. As dean of the upper school, Dad took attendance for the required Sunday chapel service, a requirement from which I did not gain exemption.

In my youth, I tried every imaginable way to avoid going: pretended not to hear wake-up calls, feigned illness, constructed elaborate but unconvincing rationales for Dad's consideration.

Nothing worked.

Each Sunday I begrudged more than two blazer-and-tie hours to God: one in Sunday school, one in church.

Time dragged. I never recovered.

I'm a father now. And our young Kevin employs all the avoidance techniques I tried on Dad. He loves to complain about the hour my wife and I require him to spend at St. Mark's on the first day of the week. Among other more charitable observations he confides, "I don't understand the sermons."

I try some of Dad's lines on him.

"Listen, and learn what you can."

"Sit quietly with your thoughts."

Like me Kevin takes no solace from these suggestions.

It also doesn't help to explain how lucky he has it. We don't make him wear a coat and tie. He only goes for an hour. He never attends Sunday school.

So after exhausting the list of responses Dad used on me, when Kevin fusses about going to Mass, I lamely settle on a weak, but much simpler and clearer, response.

"Your mother says you have to go."

Shabby, I know.

As you might guess, my wife wears her stripes differently than I. Sunday Mass attendance represents neither obligation nor burden to her. For reasons that totally escape me, she *enjoys* going to church. Her week isn't complete without it.

After we had kids, I discovered, having learned the hard way not to voice public complaint, it is in the family's best interest to present a United Parental Front on the issue of Mass attendance. Like Dad, my wife—a trained listener and a professional psychologist—turns a deaf ear to reason when one broaches the topic. She remains unmoved. If it is Sunday morning, it is time for church.

In the beginning, or at least very close to it, God made wives in a way that they would hold some unalterable, undebatable opinions. And sometimes when Kevin presses, my wife ends up sounding like her father.

"As long as you're living under my roof, you'll abide by my rules," she intones.

I feel uneasy when I hear my wife, or myself, become our fathers. I feel equally uneasy when I enforce the mother's edict. Will it scar Kevin for life? Will he end up despising church?

And yet there are times I admire Kevin's stubborn stance, his self-righteous indignation. When a service extends past an hour, he taps my watch face, gazing expectantly up at me. I feel like I am looking back in time at my own impatient self.

So for the purpose of Family Solidarity, I go to church—reluctantly, as I've said, and without fuss. But there are two additional reasons.

I stood in front of the St. Mark's altar for my kids' baptisms and vowed to rear our children in the church. I feel obligated to keep my word. It's a point of honor.

I attend with Jeri and the boys and do my part. Not only do the lads go to Mass, they attend the parish school. They received their first communions and are confirmed; they sing in the youth choir and participate in youth group functions.

Second, and this may sound contradictory, I like St. Mark's and its people. Jeri and I are active members. We contribute to its financial support. I appreciate the place the church takes in the life of my family. It therefore seems totally logical that I can like the church community and still not like attending services there.

But there is a summer Sunday morning when I decide to skip church and go fishing.

On the Saturday evening before the outing, I look Kevin in the eye, inform him of my intentions and invite him to come with.

Kevin hasn't yet taken an interest in fishing. I watch his face as invisible wheels turn in his brain, performing time calculations.

It will take more time out of his day to go fishing with me.

Plus he'd have to get up earlier.

He opts for church.

I know how much he hates going. His reply feels like a dagger in my chest. Disappointed but undaunted, I set the alarm for five-thirty.

When it sounds, I consider my current comfort level and think about catching the evening rise. Then I remember I am fifty-two and not fishing nearly as much as I'd like.

Then I remember if I don't go, I have to go to church.

In short order, I'm on the road to the river, stopping along the way for an energy fix. A couple of McMuffins and a Coke.

A bright-eyed, healthy looking man of approximate middle age approaches me at the soft drink machine. He is tan and owns a sturdy build and a slightly receding hairline. He wears a snow white, short sleeve button down shirt adorned with a bright purple and gold tie. His breath fills his chest and it gives him a confident look, an expression that hints he has some secret which pleases him. He looks me in the eye and that pleases me.

"Brother, it's a beautiful day," he says with a zeal filled voice.

"Yes, sir," I respond. For some reason I add lamely, "And I'm setting a poor example for my kids. I'm skipping church and going fishing."

The man sips his drink and furrows his brow. "Well," he says, "I'm pastor to the Free at Last Bible Church and I'm preaching the Gospel this morning." He hesitates, "But I guess it's better for you to be fishing and thinking about God than it is for you to be sitting in church and thinking about fishing."

I couldn't have said it better.

I extend my hand and we shake. "Brother," I say, "I'm gonna go think about God." In a matter of minutes, I'm driving east toward a sky streaked with orange and pink.

The morning feels cool, temperatures in the fifties, the water about the same. The August banks are overgrown, thick, prolifically head high and drenched with dew. The scent of mint and fresh water fills the air. The black river cuts easily, quietly through the Kinnickinnic canyon, as it has for thousands of years.

Wading in cautiously I still startle a blue heron who croaks and flaps awkwardly away, leaving a stream of excrement as an attitudinal expression upon lift off. I tie on a #16 caddis emerger and begin to cast in silence.

Minutes later a ruby-throated hummingbird pauses at a tubular orange flower and, from four feet away, considers my casting before darting off in search of additional nectar. I cast again, mend the line and follow the fly's drift downstream, surprised to note a buck standing staunchly in the current. Water drips from his jaw and he regards me carefully with inquisitive eyes. His nose twitches as he takes in my scent and holds my gaze for more than a minute before splashing away.

At midmorning the trout begin feeding, slashing the current. I thread a Trico spinner on my leader. In a matter of minutes I begin to catch fish. Though I have fished for years and have some experience in catching trout, I still marvel when one comes to hand, awed by its vitality and brilliance.

I hold one particular trout, a firm fleshed thirteen inch beauty, its fins edged in white, a deep gold belly, sides peppered with dark blotches. Its atavistic black eye gleams brightly in the sun.

I remove the hook from the fish's jaw and hold it in the water, nosing it upstream. The fish regroups and slips from my hand, returning to the depths where it disappears.

At that moment I feel a strong connection to creation and a reverence for God I seldom feel in church.

N.B. I wrote the bones of this story twenty years ago. I don't attend St. Mark's now. There's a new priest and he's ultra conservative. Let's leave it there. Any other comment begins to be uncharitable. I've found a new church, one I wasn't really looking for, and participate actively in its life. The Faith Mennonite people have huge hearts, like our Kevin's. They do justice, love kindness and walk humbly with their God. Their faith humbles me. They "walk the talk." I feel honored they include me. I do behind-the-scenes stuff for the church. Things no one sees, often accomplished on weekdays. I do this work so that others don't need to be bothered with it. I hope it frees them to do more for the cause of equal rights and social justice. It just shows that a person with the faith life of a flea can find a way to serve.

I still don't like going to church. I didn't go today. I took Rosie-the-Springer to the park for a long walk in a light rain. We met a stony guy on the trail. He carried a smoking bundle of sage. "Check it out, man," he started, "this is sacred." I agreed and leaned into the smoke and wafted it over me.

I consider myself blessed.

P.S. Kevin loves to go to Mass. He still doesn't fish but likes to go to the river.

✳

Discovery: Fly Fishing for Warblers

@710 words

May 2002/Winter 2019

A cooler than normal spring up north interrupted the warbler migration. The birds were in a holding pattern. So the experts said.

I didn't give this serious consideration until I visited the Lower Kinni on a Saturday in May to search for hungry trout feeding on hatching mayflies.

The swallows were out in force. By the hundreds, swooping and diving under the County F Bridge, snatching emerging insects off the river's surface.

Trout fishers love swallows. They eat the same bugs trout do. What the birds take from above, trout snatch from below. And a good time to trick a trout into taking an artificial fly that you cast on the water's surface is when real ones are hatching and the fish are paying attention.

As I deliberately made my way up the thickly wooded canyon on a warmish spring day I couldn't help but notice the warblers. They flocked in legions. Everywhere. Fueling up, waiting to continue their journey, acting like teenagers, breeding their foremost instinct.

Polarized sunglasses are a fishing tool but after ten minutes of wading and casting they became an impediment to bird watching, prompting me to ponder the purpose of my river visit. Did I want to catch fish? Or watch birds?

I love to catch fish. Love solving the puzzle, convincing a trout to eat my fly. Love the pull of a trout against my line. Love connecting to a trout's wildness.

But truth told, I've birded longer than I've fished. Chickadees fed from the child sized hand I stretched out my mother's kitchen window. I strolled with her along Hollow Road to hunt for scarlet tanagers. Twenty years later as a grad school student, I bought a bird book on total impulse and toted it to the Brigantine Refuge on my first birding trip where it proved useless. Folks up and down the Eastern Seaboard had flocked to view the rare redshank, a Eurasian wader blown somewhat off course. Though not included within the pages of my book, I recorded the sighting and continue that practice into the present day. Though I've never counted the number of species I've identified, I've seen a bunch.

In later years, trout fishing won me over. I cast more and, only occasionally, focused the binocs, when I did think to bring them.

Not so on this day. The birds proved remarkable, not for the presence of any rare species but by their sheer profusion. I slid my hook into the rod's keeper loop and stowed my sunglasses in a vest pocket.

I have never witnessed such a thick, eye level collection of warblers. Hundreds of magnolias and yellow-rumpeds, almost an equal measure of yellows, dozens of redstarts, generous sightings of Wilson's, chestnut-sideds, yellowthroats and black-and-whites. All at such close range binoculars proved superfluous. As I hiked and waded upstream the warblers were never out of sight, singing with the enthusiasm of a church choir juiced on Jesus.

What remains is a collection of mental photographs.

A yellow intercepting a mayfly in midair a yard in front of my eyes.

The pair of chestnut-sideds casually rummaging in cliff base rubble as I watched over the current dividing us.

A Wilson's perching on a nearby branch and examining me curiously.

The black-and-white so intent on finding a meal in the tree bark I tapped him on the rump with my rod tip.

The glossy flash of a tree swallow as he dipped under my outstretched fly rod; the American redstart that perched on it.

Throw in an assortment of rose-breasted grosbeaks, a pileated woodpecker, a perching bald eagle, a congregation of tiny but hungry flycatchers, the phoebes, the chickadees, nuthatches, red-wingeds, goldfinches, catbirds, robins, blue jays, grackles, downy and hairy woodpeckers, myriads of song sparrows, a startled turkey, a pair of orioles in mating ballet, a small band of hummingbirds, a bold group of ruby-crowned kinglets, ever present blue herons, Canada geese, mallards, kingfishers, a lone spotted sandpiper and one startling jewel of an indigo bunting and you have a fair day of birding. Especially if you're fishing.

Which is what I ended up doing when I realized that fish were rising. The pull was magnetic. I tied on a #16 Adams and began to cast.

Carpe Diem: Cancer, the Problem with Sulfurs & Eternity's Sunrise

@3070 words
July 2012/September 2021

This story isn't about cancer but that's how it begins. Precisely at the time my wife of twenty-eight years and I took our first-ever winter vacation, booking a weeklong stay in a Gulf-front rental house on an island off the Panhandle coast. We cut the trip short when our college kid called late one evening on the unit's landline, a number we didn't know and hadn't shared with him.

"Cancer?" Jeri exclaimed.

When a guy's nut swells to the size of an egg it gets his attention pretty quick, especially when his nursing school friend strongly advises getting to the hospital, pronto. Our younger son, Kevin, casually informs his mother of pending surgery. The next day an Oregon doctor will remove a cancerous left testicle. He tells his mom not to worry. He has "absolute confidence" in his surgeon. This from a twenty-year-old who'd only discovered his condition and met his surgeon a few hours ago. In for a penny, in for a pound.

We started home before dawn, with me riding shotgun to monitor Kevin's operation by texting his University of Portland classmate, one of a handful of female friends and roommates in his immediate collegiate support network who'd escorted him to the hospital. This is in the early days of the introduction of cell phones into our sixty-something lives If I'm an electronic Luddite, Jeri's living in the Stone Age. She doesn't text and consequently accomplishes the bulk of the driving. Maybe because of the personal nature of the procedure, I express more than mild surprise when, after successful surgery, Kevin sleeps in his own off-campus bed under the watchful care of his roommates. Meanwhile, we pass a short night, dozing fitfully, in an Illinois motel.

By mid-afternoon on the following day, we'd parked on the snowy street in front of our house and, while unpacking, our neighbor's friend side-swiped our car which I then used to drive my wife to the airport. Jeri flew to Portland to look after our son for two post-surgery weeks, leaving me at home to work, fret, drink too many IPAs and get the body work done on our car.

Since seventy-plus inches of Minnesota snow had turned our back yard into a kind of tundra, I used my free time to excavate impressive clearance trenches around the garage, rationalizing the project as a way of keeping spring melt out of the foundation. In truth? I needed to work my yah-yahs out. I moved boatloads of snow for no real reason.

The surgeon claimed he'd gotten the cancer early and advised holding off on the standard chemotherapeutic follow-up treatment. So Kevin remained in school, submitted to regular blood tests and, after switching a couple of courses to pass-fail, went about completing his junior year, proceeding at a normal pace down the graduation path.

After Jeri returned to Saint Paul, we mostly kept our worries to ourselves and breathed sighs of relief as blood tests continued to prove negative. Gradually, we relaxed. I spent four early-April days on Montana's Bighorn River and learned to fish streamers and that "the tug is the drug." Locally, I landed some nice trout on a favored section of the Root near Preston. Then the Kinni regular season opened and, well, that's home water. I love that river. And live for the sulfur hatch, an event foreshadowed by the appearance of the Dame's rocket wildflowers.

In June I fished into the evening, casting for a half hour over moving water boiling with feeding fish. Amazing. Especially in the soft, fading late spring light. A Great horned owl hoots, a doe and fawn drink warily in midstream, a muskrat ferries a mouthful of vegetation across the current, cedar waxwings lurk in river-side trees and swoop after fluttering mayflies. It's a spiritual experience, the silence reverential. But I've discovered the sulfur season brings trouble.

It started in the late nineties, when I felt faint while working at the upper Midwest's largest street fair. Summarily ambulanced off in front of gaping festival-goers, I was subsequently hooked to a hospital heart monitor, released within the hour, then walked three miles home and received an eight-hundred-dollar ambulance bill for a one-mile ride. "Stay off the river for a while," was the advice I heard. So much for the last sulfurs of the twentieth century.

I missed the following season after wiping down the ash gunwale of my canoe and impaling my finger with a toothpick-size splinter. When my arm swelled to alarming proportion, a youngish Urgent Care physician anxiously probed the wound, sterilized and bound it tightly, and ordered a tetanus shot. "Thees ees not good," she remarked with Slavic intonation. "Eef eet swells more go to Emergency Room. They have surgeon there." I didn't do a good job of fishing left-handed that year but at least I didn't need a surgeon.

I went out for sulfurs a year later even though I didn't feel up to snuff. I'd learned by then that sulfurs don't wait on a body. After I went to bed that night I did a James Brown and woke up in a cold sweat. You could still see a doctor when you needed to in those days and Doc Swen found spots on my lung. "Pneumonia," she pronounced. To hasten recovery, I cancelled an East Coast family trip while another sulfur season slipped away.

I did fish a glorious hatch that subsequent June. On arriving home I found a note to call my brother. He'd admitted my disoriented and demented father (his stepfather) to the hospital. The next day, I flew east to give Dad permission to die. In all? Bad news seems to come with the sulfurs. I don't know why.

Kevin didn't come home after completing his semester. He headed to LA and volunteered at a Catholic worker soup kitchen and hospitality house for the homeless. He's got a big heart. So with Kevin newly and safely arrived in LA, I drove off the fish the sulfurs.

Jeri's typically abed by the time I return from evening fishing. That night she and our new rescue dog, Rosie-the-Springer, met me at the door, one unabashedly wagging a stumpy tail, the other clearly crestfallen. The human in the pair offered no verbal preamble. "Kevin's coming home tomorrow. He needs to do the chemo." My wife's voice broke as she said it.

Kevin was relaxing on the beach when the Portland doctor's call came through, only three days after arriving at the Ammon Hennacy House. The bloodwork wasn't good. The cancer'd come back. Get your butt back to Portland or go home, the doc directed. But either way, do the chemo.

The timing totally pissed Kevin off. "I'd've rather fucked up my last semester by doing the chemicals than have it screw up my summer," my younger son responded to my expressed opinion about fortuitous timing, that treatment wouldn't interfere with classes or with graduating the following June.

Hell, I was just trying to cheer him up. It's all a matter of perspective.

And who was I to argue with his perspective? "My cancer's totally curable," he growled. "I'm lucky."

Lucky?

Kevin genuinely liked Dr. Mulvey, a nice Irish guy who biked and hoped to learn to fly fish Idaho. Our boy didn't flinch when informed about putting pure poison in his blood stream for the better part of nine weeks, that some days he'd feel like shit, that he'd lose his hair along with his appetite. And Jesus, all of those things happened, including waking up one morning to a hair-covered pillowcase. After he stepped out into the hall and casually pulled hanks of hair from his scalp, I went out and got a buzz cut in solidarity, a style that didn't do me any favors. But my appearance didn't affect my fishing. I didn't wet a line all summer.

"Daddy, you should go fishing," Kevin often said.

"I'm not leaving," I said back. I stayed home to offer quiet support. I did what I could to help, what I thought was needed. I don't know if it was but I did it anyway and, more often than not, that meant cooking for him and a sympathetic network of friends who gathered around our table. I got very familiar with the Whole Foods cooler where they stocked the grass-fed bison. If your kid asked for expensive chemical free meat because he's already putting enough poison into his system, you'd buy the grass-fed too.

So Kevin did the chemo and it sucked. We didn't share the news with many. But anyone who saw us in public knew the deal. A bald and pale six-three white kid with bags under his eyes and a haggard look? We got a lot of furtive stares and people averted our gaze when we caught them at it. And the few I told? To a person each shared a family cancer story.

The bad news is cancer is that pervasive. The good news is the chemical cocktails worked. Kevin's blood markers quickly returned to normal and stayed there. The better news is the course of treatment owns a lengthy track record of proven success. Kevin's now a cancer survivor. In late August, shiny-domed and debilitated, he left for his senior year at U Portland. Last thing he said to me? "Now you can go fishing."

A week later, Jeri's mom decided she'd had enough of living on her own. Alone and talking to guys coming out of the walls of her Florida double-wide, she reported a willingness to take her dead husband's advice to come and live with us. So what if she was eighty-nine, needed a new knee and hip, couldn't hear and talked to the mysterious "mean guys" who visited her at night and turned off her air conditioning? So what if the bathrooms in our modest home are located on the lower and upper levels and require stairway access? So what if she refused to sleep in a bed, electing instead to recline in a Bean Adirondack chair we set up as a part of a bedroom arrangement in our basement family room? So what if that's where I put the flat screen I finally broke down and bought to watch the Series? So what if I listened to the Cardinal victory on the Web while Mary and her daughter watched old time musicals in the basement?

"You should go fishing," my wife said.

"No way," I said. I cooked the meals, did the laundry, kept the house in order. You know, the general behind-the-scenes stuff. I did what I could to care for my wife's mom. I did what I could to care for my wife. This isn't bragging. Any guy worth his salt would do the same. Do what needs doing. Maybe I felt I needed to act the way I did because my wife by far out-earned me. I don't know. And my psychologist wife was wise enough to stay mum on that topic. "You should go fishing," she said.

Finally, I relented and planned an early October run to the Bighorn, arranged to meet a guide at Polly's, reserved a room at the dumpy Fisherman's Quarters and packed my bags.

Two days before departure Jeri woke me at 6:15 a.m. "Help," she entreated. "It's Grandma."

Mary'd tipped over on her way to the bathroom sometime in the night, could have been on her hands and knees anywhere from five minutes to five hours. No way she could tell us. All I knew is I hurt her when I grabbed her around the waist and hoisted her to her feet. No way around the pain, pain worth the price of standing.

I cancelled the Montana trip. Jeri did not object. When I occasionally talked to Kevin on the phone he offered, "You need to go fishing."

The situation did improve. I managed one afternoon on the last day of the trout season on the Root at my favorite Corn Field Run. Fishing proved slow under a high, bright sky but a couple of decent fish took the olive bugger I used as I worked my way downstream. About 4:00 the gods smiled on me. I ran into a small pod of risers and caught a beautiful brown with a perfectly presented cast, the three-weight pulsing pleasantly.

This is it, I thought. End the season on an artfully placed cast and a solid take. Then another fish rose, this one bigger than the one I'd released.

Well, one more cast. It worked. Another nicer one rose against the cliff wall. *I guess good things come in threes?* Three casts, three trout. A good way to end a season that never was but was, nevertheless, memorable.

Eventually Mary underwent a successful hip replacement and we made a Thanksgiving run to see Kevin while the Long Island brother-in-law came to live in our house to care for his mom and Rosie-our-dog. Out west in Portland, we listened to Kevin snivel and whine and complain about the things most college kids complain about, a legitimate sign of restored health and vigor. He sported a head of hair, a mini dark brown Afro, his pale skin accentuating a multi-ethnic appearance which occasionally drew racist slurs from rednecks driving pick-ups as he walked in the St. John's neighborhood. "Hey, Jew boy."

What makes a person say something like that?

In December, we moved Mary into a lovely apartment alongside a group of retired Irish nuns. Perfect placement for a woman who recites the Rosary several times a day. She had knee replacement surgery shortly thereafter. We experienced one of the mildest winters in recorded Minnesota history. I ran the snow blower once while conducting a November test-start which went much better after I opened the fuel line. No need to build a head-high mountain of snow beside our garage. Things continued to improve and, in May, we traveled west to watch Kevin graduate, with honors.

We returned home to advanced spring weather, a minimum of two weeks ahead; I had no idea how to predict the sulfurs.

And you wondered where the sulfurs had gone, didn't you? Thought I'd lost track of the story thread?

The bugs came on in mid-May and I met Pete B on the Kinni where we fished into the sunset at the No Trespassing pool. But there's always a problem with sulfurs. Torrential rain turned the river to chocolate milk.

The sulfurs never did come back the way I'd hoped, though I did find them on the Rush one June evening in a pool I call Borden's Favorite, a southwesterly run along a canyon wall. Frustratingly enough, they refused drift after drift, fly after fly, until I caught on to a technique I'd forgotten. Skitter the fly, make it appear to struggle, dance it on the surface. The strikes proved furious. Trout savaged my flies. Some of the ones who missed completely cleared the water. A lovely evening.

Then the rains returned. As the light continued to lengthen toward

Solstice, the water stayed quiet at sundown. Another year, another hatch gone. *Ephemerella Dorothea* says it all. The sulfurs are as beautiful and delicate as the feminine name suggests. And we all know about the ephemeral part. Here today. Gone tomorrow. You don't need to know Latin to know that. Like fishing reports everywhere. "You shoulda been here last week."

Kevin is due home from college tomorrow—from Portland by way of Nicaragua and Guatemala. It's a long story but we approach the three longest days of trouting at twilight, from the day before to the day after the Solstice. I hope to fish at least two of those days.

The problem is the sulfurs won't be there, though that's not the problem at all. I'm the problem, not the bugs. I'm the one forever ascribing negative associations to them.

Please teach me to hold the moment, to "seize the day," to relish the present, to learn to be grateful for what I'm given and let the rest go. "He who binds himself to a joy Does the winged life destroy." That's wisdom from William Blake, a nineteenth century English Romantic poet. I've gotta learn to take the lesson to heart.

"He who kisses the joy as it flies Lives in eternity's sunrise." Just like the kid who told me he's lucky to have contracted cancer.

✳

Serendipities

"Open skies, ready smiles, and paths to nowhere
were the best roads to friendship that he knew.
Especially when they converged at water."
Keith McCafferty, Cold Hearted River, 2017

The Sheriff's Pool

@980 words
June 2017/May 2019

One of the dumbest things I ever did was move over a thousand miles to coach small time women's basketball at an upper Midwest college where the juxtaposition of the institution's name with the word *athletics* is an oxymoron. This is a school with a record for football futility, fifty consecutive losses. At least I had the sense to form a close working relationship with a young Admissions counselor, a ploy to encourage his department to admit smart girls who could shoot. It's no surprise my effort yielded scant results—and ended in a failed career—but the counselor and I forged a friendship and we went fishing. That's one of the smartest things I ever did.

One spring afternoon almost thirty years ago John Powell invited me to explore the Chosen Valley waters of his youth. They hadn't laid out the riverside bike path yet but we read a sign posted in the grassy parking lot by the entry to a two-track that led to the stream: *No Motor Vehicles Past This Point.*

"It's not really illegal to drive in," John confided, "but the sheriff fishes here. He posts the sign to keep others out."

We didn't drive in that day but rather hiked to the river and covered a productive stretch of water I christened the *Cornfield Run*. It's an attractive and shaded mile-long length of riffles and pools and holes set against limestone cliffs and paralleled by a generously buffered farm field alternately planted annually in corn or soy beans.

Guess what was sown that year?

John and I enjoyed a great day. We caught trout. We drank a couple beers, smoked cigars and talked Guy Talk. Despite our decade-plus age difference we cemented a friendship. An easy thing to do for guys who like to fish and drink, smoke and tell stories.

Then John met a girl. He abandoned his job for a law school degree, married and moved to eastern Wisconsin for work. The couple started a family and Life in America consumed them. It's a familiar story. I know it.

We gradually lost touch but I regularly returned to that Chosen Valley river. After they paved the bike trail that snaked along it, I pedaled downstream, wader-clad, and explored additional water. I like to think I know it pretty well now. At least I can catch a trout or two.

I'm especially fond of a pool at the very head of the Cornfield Run, one John and I cast over that first afternoon. It's a wider piece of moving water that's beautiful and trouty. I typically fish it to start—or end—the day. One April afternoon I hit it *just right*. I remember retreating to the river bank, sated after catching more trout on dries than I cared to count, and thinking: *This is probably the best fishing I'll see all year.*

My supposition turned out to be true. It didn't stop me from fishing.

About seven years ago my friend Pete B *needed* to go fishing. Among other things he wanted to process his anxieties about upcoming prostate surgery. Fishing helps with that. I took Pete to my favorite river.

Pete's a fishing junkie to begin with but the river hooked him good. We've fished it more than once since then but on that first occasion I felt profound disappointment when, at the end of our day, we approached my favorite pool and found it occupied by an older man.

I'd scarcely expressed my disappointment when the stranger proved a gentleman. He spotted us, reeled in and backed out of the river, nonverbally ceding the run to us.

It didn't take long to notice hatching caddis flies. It took even less time to notice rising fish. Pete required scant encouragement. He surrendered to the moment. Easy to do when trout are rising.

While Pete cast I approached the man and thanked him for sharing. We tarried and chatted and watched Pete fish, applauding his hook-ups. As we swapped tales and shared personal data, I discovered my new friend fished this spot frequently when he served as the Fillmore County sheriff, a role he currently filled for a Twin Cities-area municipality.

I wondered if he'd posted the *No Motor Vehicles* sign Powell mentioned but the fleeting thought got lost in the conversation.

Eventually the man departed and Pete and I fished until dark. When we left that night we christened the run to honor the gracious peace officer. *The Sheriff's Pool.*

The following day I searched the Web and sent an e-mail message thanking Burnsville Sheriff Don Gudmundson for his kind gesture and for the pleasant conversation. He replied in kind. We left it at that.

Two years ago John Powell returned to the Twin Cities and opened a college placement business. In time we revisited the water that cemented our friendship and renewed the same as we caught up on each other's life. John hadn't seen, let alone fished, his home river in more than twenty years.

He noticed the rusted sign by the two-track in the parking lot and repeated his story about the cagey sheriff. John's become an avid biker so he approved of the paved trail and the easier fishing access it afforded. We mounted up and pedaled in.

I delighted in reintroducing my friend to his home water and in putting him in places where he caught trout. I saved the Sheriff's Pool for last, the one he'd first introduced to me more than a quarter century ago. Of course I *had* to share the tale about my encounter with the sheriff whose name I had forgotten. It's a good story, right?

When I uttered the word *sheriff* John interrupted. "Don Gudmundson?"

I immediately recognized the name.

"Yeah, how'd you know?"

"I was a kid when Don Gudmundson first brought me and my brother here to fish."

N.B. *From a May 27, 2017 article in the Minneapolis Star Tribune: "Longtime sheriff adds fourth Minnesota county to his list." Stearns County officials appointed Don Gudmundson, the former sheriff of Dakota, Steele and Fillmore counties, "to fill out the remainder of the term of John Sanner, who retired as sheriff in April."*

I shared this story with Sheriff Gudmundson and he replied and thanked me for the note: "Of course I remember that day. I should tell you I have had some fifty-plus trout days on that river stretch on caddis and Adams."

I read the sheriff's note to John Powell. "Don always did like to exaggerate a fishing story," he remarked with a smile.

✳

Bullet Holes, Skinny Water & Penn State Football

@2000 words

November2007/May 2019/Traver Award Entry April 2021

How many stories do you tell that are really true? Ones where you don't embellish at least a detail or two? And when you do tell a true one, you add a line at the end to certify its accuracy. I'm telling you that up front now. This is a true story. I've changed a few names to protect the innocent. Not all of them, though. That would ruin it.

Since I've fished with flies for trout for the better part of six decades, it's not surprising this one happens on a trout river. I won't presume to brag about my technical expertise or replay the catch of a trophy trout. Anyone who's fished for any length of time understands that often what we love about fishing is not the catching. It's about what happens on the water as a result of being there. Of being in the right place at the right time.

This one happened before cell phones and Wi-Fi arrived in Fort Smith, Montana. When it was a much better place to visit. We'll get to that last part in a bit. Jim will explain. Although he's not the story's central character, you should know him because the techniques he taught me put me on the river where the main event happened. And what happened there, happened in the hearts of men. This is a story about human connections and the pain of loss. I don't know why river banks tend to be places where lovely, serendipitous events occur, but they do. They're worth celebrating. To do so, I'm turning back the clock.

◈

My motel room door has two bullet holes in it. If I'd straddled the frame facing out at the time of the shooting, the upper trajectory would've passed immediately south of my crotch while the other would've creased my right ankle bone.

I don't need this additional speculation. I'm already at sixes-and-sevens in an end of the road western town when my bewhiskered guide shows up more than an hour late. As I step onto my cabin porch to greet my tardy host, I zip my sweater to the neck, consider the late October chill, the low gray sky, a forecast of snow and my personal disquietude while extending a cordial hand.

Jim owns working man's paws. Leathery. He launches our conversation somewhere from the middle of a train of thought whose antecedents I'm not privy to. "I quit guiding Orey-gun," the grizzled ghillie confides as we stand adjacent to the beleaguered door. "Got goddam Californicated. Left wingers, liberals. Jesus." He spits some chew.

Unsure how to respond, I nod my head and produce a flask. Maybe he'd like a snort? The moment feels appropriate. I swig and hand it over.

"Just the ticket," he comments dryly. "Pick-me-up'll do me good." He mutters a few apologetic and uncomplimentary words about a recalcitrant pickup and having to borrow one to tow his boat to keep our date. He glugs, Adam's apple bobbing, returns the flask, swipes his mouth with a sleeve. Then he stretches and ponders Fort Smith's spare surroundings. A dusty, weed filled parking lot; a worn, eclectic collection of trailer homes; the motley cluster of fly shops hunched in the shadow of a rusting water tower.

"The end of the fuckin' road," he remarks from beneath a black cowboy hat decorated with a plain silver band.

He can wear it.

I wouldn't dare.

"That's why I came here," he offers. "You only come here 'cause you mean to. Road don't go no further."

I omit mentioning the profit he accepts from a generous smattering of Californicated-type liberals who pay his guide fee while Jim swings an imaginary shotgun at a trio of squawking Sandhill cranes. "Bam."

He eyes me skeptically and I wonder what he sees. "If they was pelicans I'd definitely give 'em a taste of lead poisoning. Trout killin' bastards they are. Bad for bidness." He pauses and relieves me of the flask. "'Nother?"

A rhetorical question posed while twisting the cap. "Decent stuff," he remarks, "malted barley, not corn?"

"Yes," I confirm.

I can name it. Define its single malt heritage. But I remember the holes in the door, that I stand at the end of the fucking road with a man who despises liberals and poisons pelicans with high velocity lead. I figure the fancy whiskey links me with the Californicaters he detests and let him fill the silence.

"Hope you're ready to learn," he offers. "We're gonna do some wadin'. Row from spot to spot and fish the river from the water. I ain't one of those goddam Orvis Rowback Boys. Those guides fish you outta the fuckin' boat and you end up watchin' a bobber all day. When you catch a fish, they row you back over the same spot. Catchin' more trout makes for a better tip. That ain't fly fishin'." He nods to the truck. "Get your gear and climb in. Let's roll."

He neglects to ask if I have a license. I do.

Jim converts his tardiness into lemonade with a simple turn of phrase. "Bein' late won't hurt us this time of year," he asserts. "Besides, the other guys'll be downriver when we put in. More water to fish."

We spend an enjoyable October day, casting carefully in selected riffles and flats and channels, running Pheasant Tails over drop-offs, hooking trout in a light snow, warming before a portable heater, taking additional flask samplings. On occasion we pass other wading fishers and Jim comments, "Dumbasses are standin' where the fish were."

So I learn to keep my boots dry. To locate trout in shallow, moving water. And how to take them out of it.

"You're my last gig," Jim comments. We pass the communal flask and quietly consider the setting sun before Jim breaks the spell. "I'll be guidin' Florida next week."

I'm not a particularly bright guy, but I am a good learner. The older I get the better I remember lessons that matter. I've successfully employed Jim's advice any number of times since that day. And that brings me to the heart of the story.

◈

Three years hence I've rented a room behind the same bullet scarred door. I am fishing the Autumnal equinox and working my way upriver from the Three Mile landing, fishing a Ray Charles behind a San Juan worm in water barely deep enough to drown in.

I'm hiking between spots when I notice an older man, a rotund fellow with a fringe of white hair curling around the edges of a Penn State football cap. His rod vibrates in a pleasing arc. He's playing a splashy rainbow in boot deep water. "Lend a hand?" He extends his landing net toward me.

We stoop, shoulder to shoulder, over the netted fish and he revives and releases the startlingly bright animal. We are brothers.

We chat afterward and I play the role that fits. Uninformed, curious, polite.

The rosy complexioned man speaks confidently about catching fish. Montana trout, Oregon steelhead, Alaska salmon. He gestures at the water.

"Try it here? I haven't fished it out. I'm heading upriver." He points to the top of the run, "Cast up there into the shallows. Rig a Ray Charles under a San Juan."

When I turn my rod to display my brace of flies, he smiles. "You'll catch 'em up," he says confidently. "Especially if you don't go in the water. They're in the shallows."

We share our goodbyes, each pleased with the contact. As he starts walking away I toss a stray fly onto the conversation's surface. I'm curious if he knows anything about Penn State football or simply wears the hat.

I gesture at his cap when I say, "Penn State, huh? My cousin played football there for Rip Engle in the early sixties. I saw him play a couple of times and I've rooted for the Nittany Lions ever since."

The man's mouth drops open. He cocks his head and measures me with a questioning gaze. "Rip Engle? One of Rip's assistants was a guy named Joe Paterno." He asks my cousin's name.

I tell him.

He replies, "Frank Hershey was my fraternity brother." Then he points across the river to a companion tucked against the inside edge of a chute. "See that guy over there? Him, too."

Perry Ellison is a resident of Washington State. He manages a sales route for Cleveland Gear and is examining retirement with a magnifying lens. For the last several equinoxes he's rendezvoused with a few buddies at the 'Horn for a week's fishing.

He speaks fondly of my cousin and enjoys hearing my boyhood remembrance of Frankie dropping his trousers to reveal Valentine's Day heart-studded underwear to his blushing girlfriend. Frankie, the high school quarterback star of his Lancaster McCaskey team the year they won the Central Penn title. An era when the Pennsylvania Friday night lights shone particularly bright.

Perry'd kept touch with my cousin. More than I ever did, given our age difference and geographic dislocation. He recites Frank's post-graduation coaching pedigree, taking me from Norwich to Franklin & Marshall to Millersville to Dartmouth to Harvard and back to Hanover. He pauses and sighs and looks away. We hold a long measure of reticence as the river and remembrance speak.

"I miss him," Perry whispers.

I honor the moment with silence.

Frank Hershey died of cancer nine years ago, on October 15, a victim of non-Hodgkin's lymphoma.

A few moments later we restate our goodbyes and Perry points to the rapid. "Stay out of the water," he advises before he turns away.

The river flow barely wets my boot soles when I land two bright bellied browns in the next three casts. They took the Ray Charles.

◈

The following Monday morning a crewcut, unshaven man of Italian heritage eases onto the Billings-to-Minneapolis dawn patrol as the flight attendant is closing the cabin door. He fills the last seat on the plane. Next to me.

He sports a long sleeve tee emblazoned with a leaping rainbow trout. He's *that guy over there*. The fisherman Perry pointed to during our encounter.

Joe Giordano is a Jersey guy. He belonged to Phi Delt with Frank and Perry, spent twenty years in the Navy, last stationed in Connecticut at the New London sub base. Now he lives in nearby Gales Ferry. He still works but, like Perry, is looking eagerly and seriously at retirement.

He calls Frank *the Hawk*. He tells me stuff I know.

Frankie played *both ways*. At running back and safety before settling in at punter and defensive back. He earned All-East honors in a time when teams still valued winning the Lambert Trophy.

Joe also tells me stuff I don't know. About how well Frank played in the Gator Bowl when Penn State defender David Robinson "destroyed Georgia Tech."

Joe remembers Franks' wife, the embarrassed teenager to whom Frank displayed his Valentine's Day drawers. "She was a beautiful woman." Then he looks at me slyly. "Hawk coulda had any girl he wanted."

It's the kind of thing guys who couldn't have any girl they wanted remembered.

"I had a cousin who came down from Elmira for a weekend. First thing she does is point at Hawk and ask, 'Who's that handsome guy?' I told her he was taken."

We shake in the Minneapolis airport. "You don't have to stay in the motel with the bullet holes in the door if you don't want," Joe proposes. "Meet us for equinox week and you can bunk with us at Cottonwood Camp."

Whether I accept the invitation or not it is comforting to know that the memory of a favorite and admired cousin—the boy child of my departed father's elder brother—a loving husband and father, a talented coach and a man of substance who loved country music who continues to live so vividly in the minds of his friends and who, for a moment, lived again at the edge of the Bighorn River.

N.B. *Frank Hershey was a three-year Penn State letterman as a defensive back and punter and played in the 1962 Gator Bowl. In 1964 he was named All-East and received honorable mention All-America recognition. He began his coaching career in 1965 as an assistant at Norwich University (VT) and filled roles as an admissions representative, assistant athletic director and business manager. He then coached at Franklin & Marshall College and at Millersville State (PA) before earning an appointment to the Dartmouth College staff where he coached running backs and receivers for five years, including the 1981 and 1982 Ivy League championship teams. In 1987 he moved to Harvard University, where for seven years he served as running backs coach. Frank returned to Dartmouth in 1994 to coach the receivers and running backs. He was a part of the Dartmouth's 1996 Ivy League championship team that finished 10-0 and ended the season ranked 17th in the nation. He was a member of the American Football Coaches Association,* *serving on the association's Assistant Coaches Committee and was elected to the athletic hall of fames at Norwich University and at J.P. McCaskey High School (PA) where he was an All-State quarterback. He died October 15, 1998. He was fifty-six.*

✻

An Irish Traffic Jam

@1675 words

August 2001/Fall 2018

Sean is earning money to pay for his eighth grade DC trip. He's working beside me in the garden and has excavated a trench where we will plant tulip bulbs, between the drive and east side of the front porch. The spot catches the morning sun. The stucco wall intensifies the heat by reflecting it onto the earth. The garden will produce our earliest spring blossoms, especially if we add bone meal to nourish the bulbs.

We are working the pungent fertilizer into the loosened soil when Kevin comes to the porch rail and peers over at us. He wears a grave expression.

"Mommy is on the phone with Grandma. Grandpa is dying," he says.

We put Jeri on the next plane to Tampa. The following day she watches her eighty year-old father die. My wife and her brother and mother spend the next few days attending to end of life details and Jeri comes home to announce we're taking a trip to Ireland next summer to honor her dad's final wish.

Jimmy's asked his children to return his ashes to his parents' family grave, people Jimmy knew he'd never see alive again when he and his new bride sailed for the States in 1948.

By late July of the following year the tulips have bloomed crimson, the garden is officially christened *Grandpa's Garden* and our family has rendezvoused with Jeri's brother's family in Limerick City. We've spent a handful of days with our gracious Irish family, attended a memorial Mass at St. John's Cathedral—the tallest church in Ireland and the place of Jimmy's baptism, first communion, confirmation and marriage. We've driven up Mulgrave Street, past the turnoff to the Rossa Avenue family homestead, past the greyhound park and the prison, to crowded Mt. St. Lawrence Cemetery where stones are adorned with plastic wreaths, religious icons, family photos, rosaries and vases holding wilted flowers. The headstones stand shoulder to shoulder like a garden of gray and black-and-white tulips. We've read the appropriate verses and said the appropriate prayers, deposited Jimmy's remains in a narrow plot, host to multiple family members.

A life has been commemorated and honored. We miss him. We lift pints in his memory at Jerry O'Dea's pub.

Funereal duties completed, our American families agreed to see a bit of Ireland together, a golf-centric tour of western Ireland—Lahinch and Ballybunion—as determined by my brother-in-law's interest in the sport. Now our companion family has departed for the States, leaving our foursome at *Cnoc-na-ri*, a country B&B outside of Ballymacarbry.

We take to the Comeragh Hills in south central Ireland and steer toward the famous Rock at Cashel, an imposing limestone outcrop which rises dramatically over the livestock dotted Tipperary plain. Home to a complex of ancient stone buildings, Cashel is a hallmark stop on the tourist trail, the crowded kind of place we prefer to avoid. Regardless of the throng, it is a mystical experience to wander among the stone structures, high crosses, the ninety-foot round tower, carved Romanesque archways and a multitude of gravesites. It is a peaceful and awe inspiring place. I understand why monks flocked here.

We eat a late lunch—tea, sandwiches, scones, *veg soup* and stout—in Clonmel at a small shop on O'Connell Street. By seven we've returned to *Cnoc*, a quiet mountain retreat. I am free to fish the Nire.

I've read how you must pay to fish *beats* on Irish streams. Even though my hosts provide a clearly legible fisherman's map and confidently finger access points, I wonder about the legality of my venture. No one mentions a license. But I am less concerned about that than I am about playing the Rude Yank.

I park in a wayside by the Fourmile Bridge, a stone arch spanning a bucolic waterway, gear up and walk to the bridge's apex. Two men stand in the flow. One casts a fly while the other points to holding spots. A good sign. Still slightly uneasy I slip warily through the barbed wire gate and walk away from the men.

They depart within minutes and I am alone on the water. I wander downstream through a leafy glade and emerge in pastureland where I am quite alone, removed from any busy road. The silence is comforting, audible.

There is a riffle below a tractor crossing where the current flows over a concrete slab laid across the stream bed. Trout are rising.

I tie on a #16 flying ant and hook a few small browns, a satisfactory but unremarkable experience. I am happy to be here but I remind myself of a determination to keep this a family vacation, not *Dad's Irish Fishing Tour*.

I am standing in an Irish trout stream. I have caught trout. It is enough. I head toward the car.

As I approach the bridge I encounter a flock of ducks. They barely move and, in fact, seem inconvenienced as I forge through them and scramble through a fence opening where I meet an unshaven sixty-something man with crooked teeth and a tweed hat.

We talk fishing. He is interested that I have caught some. The big fish are gone, he laments. He peers into in my fly box and I identify several he's not seen.

He no longer fishes. He keeps ducks and feeds them twice a day, which is where he is going, thus accounting for the flock's minimal reaction to my wading.

As we chat I notice Lonergran's, a pub set seemingly in the middle of nowhere. I pause and smile at my memory of Jimmy Rockett and how he enjoyed taking me out for a pint, always saying, "A bird with one wing never flew," before ordering a second. A pint in his memory is fitting.

A scroffly, belligerent pooch the size of a small footstool yaps at me and a bony redhead with pointy breasts builds a pint in a dingy bar the size of a bedroom. "Don't mind 'im," she nods at the dog. "He's needing a good boot up 'is arse."

I sit at the bar for a few uncomfortable moments among three locals—two young men and a man of my approximate vintage. Conversation arrives about the time the pint settles and we chat amiably. I am a willing fount of American knowledge.

They are curious about snow and cold weather. They lift their eyebrows when I report the negative-twenty-four reading on my back yard thermometer last winter. "Fahrenheit," I add for emphasis and they wince.

They inquire about heat and traffic. "You grew up on Long Island?" one asks. "I have friends there."

It is pointless to tell him Long Island is over a hundred miles long or that millions live there so I nod knowingly.

I order a second pint for which I am not allowed to pay and finally depart with the man of my age. We amble toward his car and he stops to look about as I continue toward the bridge and my unseen vehicle. "Are you wanting a lift?" he inquires.

I smile, nod and politely decline his offer with a wave indicating the location of my rental.

The drive to the main road follows a narrow, twisty way where, for a driver accustomed to navigating the opposite side of the middle stripe, stone walls loom ominously close to the macadam. Steering carefully around a tight turn, an Irish Traffic Jam hinders my progress.

A flock of sheep moves sedately up the thoroughfare ahead. A suspendered farmer stands behind his charges and chats with a man who has just driven head-on and slowly through the sheep. I brake gently next to them. The driver and the farmer peer inquisitively at me.

"How's the holiday?" asks the driver.

I lean out the window. "Now how are you knowing I'm on holiday?"

They laugh at my obvious joke. I am off the beaten path and clearly a tourist. American at that.

We share a few mouthfuls of pleasantries before the driver departs, leaving me with the shepherd who is disposed to talk. He allows I might have fished his land but nods his head when I mention my Ballymac hosts, Richard and Nora Harte. I cite the real reason for my Irish sojourn. The man crosses himself and says, "God rest his soul."

By this time the farmer's wife has followed the sheep around a bend and out of sight. The man accepts a lift.

As we proceed, his sheepdog becomes confused and refuses to follow. It races back to the spot where his master left the road and entered my car. The man leans out the window, calls to the hound and opens the door. The dog wags his tail, runs to us and leaps into his master's lap. I allow that we own a quasi-border collie like his.

"Aye, but mine is smarter," he says.

"Ah, but mine is fatter."

We grin at one another across an ethnic, cultural and generational divide. We have established human contact.

We regain the flock and the eager, panting dog jumps through the window to resume his work. Not subject to the dog's genetic imprint we remain content to idle slowly behind.

In a few minutes the wife clears the way, moving the animals to a right fork in the road. Though *right* is the direction I know to return to the main highway, the man points left and assures me I will find the way. He exits the car, leans back in the window, looks me in the eye and extends a leathery hand. We shake.

"It's always a pleasure to be meeting a man like you," he says. "God bless."

I am left to ponder the most memorable aspects of fishing the Nire, which have nothing at all to do with angling, and my mind drifts back to the tulips in *Grandpa's Garden* and I puzzle at the surprising sequence of events that put me on a back road in Ireland at the literal tail end of an Irish Traffic Jam.

✳

Of Grouse & the Whale

@965 words
October 2012/Winter 2019

On Sunday night I head to the Kinni with Pete B. We hike a good piece downriver and cast at sunset on a deep bend below the Crossing Pool. Pete's up at the top of the run. He's fishing the chute where the river narrows and deepens before turning hard to the northwest, running smoother and deeper until it deposits its contents into the Dartmouth Pool.

I'm below Pete standing opposite a corner where I once flipped a canoe, my nine year-old boy unable to execute a draw stroke I neglected to teach him. There's a sporadic rise. Maybe fish are taking tiny mayflies. We don't know for sure.

It doesn't matter. I've caught enough fish and I didn't bring a headlamp. At my age there's no way I'm going to try to change out a #16 caddis at dusk for a tinier mayfly. Besides, maturity has mellowed me. I've enrolled in the school of fishing where I worry less about fly size and matching the hatch and more about whether I can track my presentation and how it's hunting. So I'm skittering my deer hair bug and sometimes a trout takes it. What's not to like?

In reality, I'm hanging around until Pete B's done. He gets a trifle single-minded when he fishes. We might be here a while. I start to daydream and am gazing absently at my caddis as it starts to drag when it happens much faster than I can tell it. It is a vision forever imprinted on my brain.

An enormous fish ghosts out of the deep and flashes at the fly. When it sees the drag, or me, it quickly retreats. I've never seen a fish that size on the Kinni, one measuring in excess of excess of twenty inches. These days a twelve-to-fourteen inch trout might represent *the trout of the season.* I let out an astonished yelp.

You know I spooked the fish and didn't have a prayer of bringing it up that night. But it's a good story and, over Rush River IPAs at the Copper Kettle, Pete B and I scheme about returning one night. Run a big streamer or a mouse through the pool. See if The Whale will come out to play after dark.

Of course we don't. Go back, that is.

The season shifts and I'm visiting with a DNR officer to learn about finding grouse cover relatively local to the Twin Cities. He's organized a series of waypointed Google Earth maps and teaches me how to identify cover on them, orienting me to the finer points of the website mapping system and sharing nuggets about the cover grouse like best.

I'm in way over my head here but I do have a willing Springer who graciously withholds comment on my shooting ability so I listen.

This guy knows his onions. He's clearly happy to have someone to talk to who's interested in what he knows. He's a trained naturalist, has hired out as a hunting and fishing guide and now participates in the three outdoor activities he likes best. Grouse hunting: "You know you're where you need to be if you're in cover so thick you can't fall over." Bow hunting for deer: "I'm no trophy hunter. I take the first one I see for the meat." Trout fishing: He shows me a picture of a huge brookie on his computer desktop and tells me he makes his own bamboo rods.

His piscatorial admission triggers another ten minutes of conversation. He's a minimalist fly guy but it turns out he takes photos. Pretty soon he's clicking at fish porn on his computer screen in a sharing way that doesn't make me feel like we're comparing penis sizes.

The dude just loves what he does. He loves to hunt, fish and to tell people about it. Good for him. I'm jealous.

Next thing I know I'm looking at a photo of his friend who's holding a twenty-six inch brown trout.

"Where in Montana did he catch it?" I ask.

"He pulled it out of the Kinni earlier this year."

"No way."

"Yes, way," he insists before sheepishly confessing his friend might have *cheated* to catch it by locating it with an underwater camera.

The officer then grants the friend absolution. "He did release it, though."

You know I have to ask. "Where?"

Now I don't know this guy. Never talked to him before. But he's not the kind of guy who keeps that info to himself. It doesn't take long for him to describe the same Crossing Pool and deep bend in the river just a hundred yards downstream. The exact place I stood when I met The Whale.

JOHN HERSHEY

You know what comes next. The following Sunday I trudge downriver late and spend an agreeable half hour casting to greedy risers in the Dartmouth Pool. Just after dark I sneak upstream to the Whale Pool, shorten the leader and tie on a mouse. I briefly ponder the *On Golden Pond* bass Henry Fonda named *Walter* and start casting carefully, deliberately, and quietly in the dark and get lost in the process.

You also know the big brown doesn't take the mouse. After a lengthy wait, he doesn't take a big streamer either. He doesn't take a whole bunch of things I cast.

It's a longer walk out than usual, hot and sweaty, and darker than I've seen it. I usually don't need a light on my outbound hikes beside a river I know pretty well but this night I do. I spook a deer and more than one blue heron. A beaver slaps his tail on the water and spooks me. But the beer at the Copper Kettle sure tastes good. And I have a good story to tell.

✳

A Surfeit of Rods

@2970 words

January 2001/Winter 2019

Folks cautioned me about the cold when we moved to Minnesota. "It doesn't ice out 'til May," offered one educated soul. Another spoke plainly. "You'll freeze your balls off."

I purchased a down parka, a collection of heavy socks, polypropylene long johns and prepared for Arctic living. Once I took a shot of frostbite on the tip of my ear and understood it really can be dangerous to go hatless in subzero temperatures, winter didn't seem all that bad. The heat surprised the hell out of me.

Our second Minnesota summer recorded more than forty days of ninety-plus degree heat. The humidity felt exponentially worse. Into this sort of weather our first child, a boy named Sean, was born.

You can imagine the delight Sean's maternal grandparents expressed upon the arrival of their only daughter's first child. A boy child given a family name to boot. They drove from Florida to visit for six weeks.

And oh yes, by the way, we thought Grandpa could get his hip replaced at the Mayo while we're in town? You don't mind if we install a hospital rent-a-bed in your dining room for his recuperation, do you? We know you're painting the house and you have a new baby, but we really won't be a bother...

The in-laws arrived and moved in for protracted convalescence. Painters swarmed the house, sealing off windows as they proceeded around our central air-free home. Though Baby Sean's colic necessitated extra care, Grandma remained a loving care assistant and provider. Her presence rendered my willingly offered support superfluous. Meanwhile the fussiest baby in the house proved to be a convalescing seventy year-old Irishman with a metal hip. The heat wave continued. I *needed* to go fishing.

I drove to the Whitewater and happened into a splashy evening rise on the North Branch just below a concrete bridge which barely lifts the road over the river's flow. At dark I stopped for two quick drafts and an equal number of spiced, hard-boiled eggs at my all-time favorite Minnesota joint: Mauer's. A dim, outdoorsy bar, its walls festooned with dusty mounts of multiple species. A huge turkey. A giant brown. The "biggest trophy of the week" board hung by the door. A smoked country atmosphere thick enough to spread.

And so, after a brief foray into Sanity, I returned to Saint Paul and the reality of caring for young and old babies, of tiptoeing around a sensitive mother-in-law's feelings, of ninety percent humidity in a house smelling of oil base paint.

I'm not sure why my wife loves me but I ask no questions. I love it that she doesn't fuss when I go fishing. Over the next few days, although confident I didn't need to do my fair share of chores to earn more river time, I did them anyway. I held my tongue, played the obedient son-in-law, found the appropriate opening to return to the river and headed to the basement to retrieve my rod which I stored in the northwest corner rafters, a place I'd mentally catalogued as the fishing and tying room I hadn't quite built.

The rod and its tube were not there.

After checking and rechecking the rafters, I searched out places I knew in my heart of hearts I would never leave my rod: the garage, the back of the Jeep, assorted closets, under beds. I must've left the rod at the Whitewater.

How could I have left my favorite, and only, rod behind? The one my friend Coach Flyfish built for me?

◈

Three winters earlier I sat on a couch in Coach Flyfish's Rochester, NY living room determined to spend the first money I'd earned through writing on a legitimate fly rod Coach Flyfish agreed to make. First we had to figure out what kind of blank to order.

Flyfish's father did business in the tackle industry and the son owned the equipment to prove it. He disappeared regularly into his tying room, emerging with rod after rod, enthusiastically describing their personalities as he handed each to me. I bet I held more than two dozen rods in my inexperienced hands.

What weight? What action? How long? I didn't know they made different style grips.

I became thoroughly confused and the pot didn't help. They mostly felt the same.

In the end, I liked the Fisher best. Coach Flyfish called and ordered the requisite parts. A two-piece, eight-and-a-half foot, five-weight blank to be fitted with a rosewood seat, a full wells grip and an aluminum rod case. I felt secret delight that we included an amenity as insignificant as a hook keeper. Purchasing the rod and its fixings made me feel I'd just gained entry to some esoteric fraternity. It added legitimacy to my self-definition as a fisher with flies.

In the spring, Flyfish sent me the finished product. A handsome, finely crafted rod, stylish and understated, inscribed with my name and completion date: 5/14/86.

Absolutely delighted, I used it regularly. It more than adequately served my limited fly fishing abilities. Now I'd lost it.

I called Mauer's and Jonny's bar across the way. Did anyone turn in a rod in an aluminum case? Then I tried the office at nearby Whitewater Park. The rod had my name on it, I offered helpfully.

No dice.

After another futile house search, I faced the cold hard facts. In the excitement of Sean's arrival and the subsequent distraction of heat and in-law invasion, the paint fumes went to my head. I'd lost my fly rod.

I *had* to buy a new one.

I drove to Minneapolis on a steamy Saturday afternoon, to the only fly shop I knew, a place on Grand Avenue, Bright Waters, owned by a kind, bushy eyebrowed ex-newspaperman. Tom Helgeson possessed the grace to withhold comment on my limited fishing sophistication. He happily showed me a collection of beginner rods.

I tried a few Cortlands in the eighty-to-hundred dollar range. They seemed okay but didn't feel like the missing Fisher. Then I picked up an Orvis six-weight, one from a Green Mountain beginner kit. Tom set me up with a reel and a ratty line and sent me out to the deserted avenue for a few test casts. Maybe I liked the action or maybe I liked the idea of the Orvis name. Whatever the cause, I *wanted* that rod.

I felt decadent for considering an Orvis, a splurge for a father with limited income and a young child. Particularly for two hundred bucks. But then I eased my conscience a bit by rationalizing the purchase as a good deal because it also included a reel and fly line in the bargain. Backing, too.

Tom clinched the deal. "Orvis rods come with lifetime guarantees. You break one on the stream, slam it in a car door, step on it? They'll fix it for free."

Why not? The rod had a keeper and even came with a case, albeit a chintzy plastic one.

Jeri didn't flinch when I shared the cost, a champagne acquisition on a beer budget kind of decision. Maybe she was distracted by caring for our colicky boy, or by the heat or the paint fumes or her needy parents. Maybe she's just good at what she does.

She's a psychologist.

I happily used the Green Mountain for the remainder of the trout season.

In the fall, I was standing on a step ladder, fussing in the basement rafters with the pipe valves that lead to the furnace overflow tank in the southeast corner of the house when I noticed an aluminum rod case tucked neatly against the ceiling there.

Coach Flyfish's rod.

I'd stored it in the rafters diagonally opposite from my mental fishing room. To this day I don't know why I put it there. Best I can figure is to chalk it up to the general insanity brought on by a collection of life stresses. A new baby. Our first child. Needy in-laws. Paint fumes. The heat. But delight outweighed any sense of general chagrin I felt. Absolutely pleased to find the Fisher, I assigned the Green Mountain to a backup role.

The Fisher became an old friend over the decade I used it. Then I skipped out of work on a soft May afternoon, the anniversary of the completion of Flyfish's rod, and headed to the Kinnickinnic River.

I habitually hike downstream from the River Ridge access but for some odd reason I turned upstream toward the dam that day and walked into a wonderful hatch of Blue-winged olives. In a matter of minutes I hooked several fish until…SNAP!

The rod tip broke in mid cast. About six inches from the top.

As pure angst filled my gut, fish continued to rise so I soldiered on. Coaxing adequate service from the damaged tool, I managed to catch a couple more before returning to the car. When push came to shove, the Fisher served me to the end and, once more, the Green Mountain was elevated to the first string.

In the aftermath of the Fisher Rod Disaster that fall, the Green Mountain didn't feel right. I'd like to think years of practice had sensitized my casting touch, that I now required a more responsive rod, but I knew that wasn't the case. In reality, it was a psychological issue. My pride bested me. The Green Mountain was a Beginner's Rod and I was no longer a beginner.

I started saving for a new rod.

◈

I didn't expect Aunt Betty to die. And I'm totally surprised she named me in her will. It's a long story. What's germane here is the inheritance provided sufficient flexibility to afford just a little more than a new retaining wall for the driveway.

With Bright Waters long defunct, I took my business to a new shop, Summit Fly Fishing, ironically situated on another Grand Avenue, this one in Saint Paul, whereupon I made the most extravagant fly fishing purchase of my life. Paul Mueller sold me a Sage, an eight-and-a-half foot, five-weight, and I began a relationship with a new fly rod whose action and casting pleased me no end.

In March, I attended a Tom Helgeson-initiated trout fishers' show where guides and outfitters passed parts of their winters drumming up trade. Then I constructed the perfect e-mail and sent it to a Baltimore friend, a paddler not without skill. Walt seized my query like a hungry brookie and we determined to fish the Bighorn and Missouri from my canoe in July.

A match made in heaven. Walt loves to paddle. I love to fish. He flew to Minneapolis and we drove west.

We idled below the Yellowtail Dam and I tossed a hopper to the river banks with delightful success. When I reminded Walt about an outfitter's cautionary tale to avoid the only dangerous spot on the stretch of the Bighorn we planned to run, a suck hole of some proportion, Walt scoffed at the warning. He paddled directly at it. "I take shits bigger than this rapid," he boasted.

I'm certain there's a twofold cause behind our capsizing: *hubris* and the fact that Walt packed his cell phone. Whatever the cause, my Sage disappeared. So did the cell phone, along with Walt's camera. The Orvis, once again, became my primary rod.

Two days later we waded the upper Missouri near Wolf Creek on a wide, braided piece below the dam. I'd never seen so many caddis flies. They were legion. On the final cast of the evening my fly snagged in heavy weed. I jerked the rod to free the line and the tip of the faithful Green Mountain broke off. Just like that.

With my watch reading nine p.m. Mountain Daylight Time, I considered my situation. I stood in one of the premier western trout rivers on a fly fishing trip without a fly rod. I had lost one and broken another. To make matters worse I'd hired my first-ever trout guide. We'd made plans to float the Missouri the following morning.

And there I was. A greenhorn without a rod.

With nothing to do but sulk we returned to Wolf Creek. At least we found a friendly tavern. Several beers and one shot later, I began to see the humor in my situation.

I rose extra early the next morning, left Walt snoozing on the floor of Frenchy's wayside motel and wandered smack down the middle of Wolf Creek's deserted main drag to an outfitter's shop, coaching myself to bear up under my complete chagrin and embarrassment. Can I please rent a fly rod?

A pretty young woman set me up with a six-weight. So what if it was a right-hand retrieve, that there was tape on the grip or that it weighed about a hundred pounds? It' was a matter of pride. I couldn't meet my guide in Craig without a rod.

The young guide put us over fish on a glorious day. We occasionally stopped to wade and the guide spent time with Walt-the-beginner while directing me to fishy spots. I was pleased to catch a rainbow *on my own* and retain a vision of it porpoising at a distance that seemed a football field away.

Though the heavy rod strained an already tender elbow, I pridefully refused Walt's offer to switch rods so I could use the Sage he bought in Hardin after we capsized. Talk about *hubris*. We fished out the day in fine style and I returned to Saint Paul and took Tom Helgeson at his word.

I called Orvis about their guarantee and a helpful service rep expressed no concern about replacing the tip. Subsequently, Mail Boxes Unlimited charged twenty bucks to ship an oddly sized parcel. Returning home, I readied the family, now one boy larger, for our annual drive to visit Florida family. Remember those in-laws?

Three weeks later, we arrived back home safe and sound. I'd caught speckled trout in Apalachicola Bay and was feeling more and more like a fisherman. In our absence Orvis had returned the rod. They'd replaced the tip section with a new one.

Two days hence, I sifted through the pounds of accumulated vacation mail and opened a letter from Orvis. The company will gladly replace the rod tip for a fifty dollar service fee. Will I please sign the enclosed form, which consents to the repair, and return it in the provided envelope? They'll then make the replacement and ship the rod.

Since I already had the rod and didn't agreed to pay the fee, I figured Orvis pitied me and simply made the exchange. I didn't return their agreement, but I did store it in a desk drawer.

A bill arrived in September. I wrote to Customer Service and described the situation. Basically, I wasn't interested in paying fifty bucks toward a fourteen year-old starter rod repair. I'd rather put the money toward a new one. I enclosed the letter, a copy of the unsigned agreement and included appropriate contact information.

When a month passed with no reply and I received another bill, I wrote again, enclosing copies of all previous correspondence.

Another month. No reply. Another bill.

Exasperated, I packed the rod and the pertinent correspondence, enclosed an explanatory note and shipped the aggregate to Orvis' Vermont address.

Please keep the rod? Give it to someone who can use it? Perhaps a youngster?

My note also didn't request reimbursement for the shipping fees and, in gentle language, I suggested I planned to consider purchasing a rod from a similar reputable company, one which will back its lifetime guarantee.

Not a threat. Merely a statement. Bottom line? I didn't like debts. I just wanted to be even.

During the week before Christmas a young woman called me at work. An Orvis rep spoke politely, expressing solicitous concern.

"Sir, y'all have a problem," she began, "and now we have one, too. We've got an unhappy customer. You're a man without a rod."

I refrained from asking how she knew about my sex life but did tell her about my fishing rod, stating I merely returned what I had not paid for and that I had no ulterior motive. I only wanted to be even.

"Would you accept a new one," she asked?

I declined, not wanting to take advantage.

"What can I do to make things right?"

"Return the Green Mountain? That would be cool."

"Oh we can't do that, sir," she said. "We've already destroyed it."

"Destroyed it?"

"Yes, sir."

Yikes.

The sincere woman continued to insist and I consented to accept a new rod as a Christmas present from Orvis. She agreed to send a nine foot Silver Label, described in the catalogue as a "mid-flex six-weight." It listed for three hundred and fifty dollars.

Though it didn't seem a fair trade, swapping a fourteen year-old starter kit rod for one twice the value, I felt content in believing I had been rewarded for nobly enduring the consequences of Walt's *hubris* in the Bighorn rapids and for his cell phone sin. As a matter of course I sent a Christmas card to the charming Southern service representative.

◈

In January a rod-shaped package arrived from Baltimore, shipped by my intrepid stern man. Walt had purchased a rod at the Bighorn Fly Shop in Hardin, a fine Sage five-weight, the day after we capsized and found ourselves one rod short for the remainder of the trip. He enclosed a brief note.

"I loved the adventure but I won't use the rod enough to justify keeping it," he related. "I still feel bad about dumping you. Please take this one as a gift. It'll make me feel better."

I now own several other higher end rods but I continue to use Walt's Sage. It is my favorite rod.

Now it's an antique.

N.B. *From the Minneapolis Star Tribune, November 17, 2010. "Tom Helgeson, a journalist turned fly-fisherman who became one of the Midwest's most prominent spokesmen for the sport and for conservation, died Friday of complications from lung cancer. He was 71." You can read more about Tom in the notation that appears at the end of "I Should Know Better" which appears in this anthology. He is also fondly remembered in "Sunday Offerings.".*

I recently gave away the faithful Sage. Fly shop guys now refer to rods from that era as a time "when Sage made good rods." I think Scott needed it more than I.

✦

Patcha

@300 words
August 2001/August 2019

A pair of hip-wadered, graying men are watching the water, waiting. The salmon are coming in with the evening tide, they say. This is Irish fly fishing on the Crana River in County Donegal. They mean to keep what they catch.

An ocean-fresh fish? I'd keep one, too. Wouldn't you?

They hold nine-weight fly rods, outfitted with sinking spey lines, tipped with ten pound monofilament, and fish down and across, paying careful attention to the deeper lies where they dangle their flies.

The elder man flips open his fly box at my request. He's tied his "flies" on #6 treble hooks. They are beautiful. Several have weighted bodies; red and orange, ribbed with fine gold wire, collared with delicate hackle.

The man extracts one, holds it up. "It's your'n." He nods at me and smiles and drops it into my open palm.

"What do you call it?" I ask before thanking him.

He utters a word I cannot cipher.

It sounds like it begins with a *P* and I incline my ear toward him, a nonverbal clue to repeat the name, which he does, drawing my puzzled expression. He repeats it once more.

"What?"

Visibly frustrated, he thinks a minute. He points to a feather in his fly box and picks up an imaginary one and holds it behind the top of his head. "Like your Injun," he says. "Patcha."

The light bulb goes on.

"Oh," I say. "Apache Indians. An Apache fly." I finish with, "Patcha."

"Patcha," he intones, his smile indicating we've vanquished the language barrier.

I thank him again and bow slightly. He nods and speaks in a brogue I cannot translate as he steps into the river.

It's probably as close as I'll get to fishing an Irish salmon run. Close enough.

Sacred Spaces

"It is important that sometime in a man's life he gets to know a place. Becomes bound up in a special piece of geography. Such a place need not be vast, exotic, brutally wild. It need only be a place that increases him, nourishes him."
Harry Middleton, On the Spine of Time, 1997

"To see and know a place is a contemplative act. It means emptying our minds and letting what is there, in all its multiplicity and endless variety, come in."
Gretel Ehrlich, "Landscape," introduction to Legacy of Light, 1987

"There is no need to personify a river: it is much too literally alive in its own way, and like air and earth themselves is a creature more powerful, more basic, than any living thing the earth has borne. It is one of those few, huge, casual and aloof creatures by the mercy of whose existence our own existence was made possible."
James Agee, Let Us Not Praise Famous Men, 1941

The Whitewater: Trinity

@1025 words
February 2015/Winter 2019

I listen for the river. For the symphony water creates as it flows over rock, a pure and clean sound and a motivating factor that sends me there to fish for trout with flies on a gray and damp morning in early November when I point the Jeep toward the Whitewater precisely because I know

I'll hear the melody the river has been playing for thousands of years as it patiently and relentlessly carves through ancient rock, opening a valley and exposing a world dramatically different than the general lay of the southern Minnesota landscape.

A little more than ten miles south and east of Plainview, Winona County Highway 26 drops and twists down Whiskey Hill into Elba, the principal town in the Whitewater valley and home to Whitewater State Park. The valley rock was laid down as calcium-based oceanic precipitates over the course of thirty to forty million years when this part of Minnesota lay under a vast shallow sea.

What I see today is what the ocean left behind. Sedimentary rock, largely limestone and sandstone, layers of compressed and cemented oceanic deposits exposed over time by riverine erosion and subsequent weathering.

Think about it in very basic terms. Drive downhill for two minutes, lose approximately three hundred feet in elevation and arrive at the valley floor. You literally roll back in time, through the Cenozoic and Mesozoic eras all the way into the Cambrian and Ordovician periods of the Paleozoic Era. From three hundred million years before the present to about five hundred million years ago.

The concept adds a peculiar mystique to the trip. It is another piece of the magic which continues to lure me to the Whitewater.

Last summer the Minnesota DNR attained a higher level of Enlightenment by adopting a regionally-based continuous trout fishing season. You can fish year 'round within the park—on parts of the Middle Branch of the Whitewater and on a tributary, Trout Run.

A uniformed park ranger highlights a map with a yellow marker, indicating pieces of the Middle Branch I haven't fished. She neatly sums up the new regulations in one sentence. "In the parks around here there are two seasons—harvest or catch and release." She adds, "It's a beautiful river."

In contrast to the valley rock, the Whitewater River is an infant, formed by glacial melt roughly between ten and seventy-five thousand years ago as glaciers advanced and retreated across the land, never quite reaching southwest Wisconsin and southeast Minnesota. The so-called Driftless Region is an area free of glacial leavings but one seriously affected by runoff. Think about a melting glacier that's hundreds of feet thick. We're talking about some serious sculpting.

I park in the shadow of a limestone cliff at the end of a gravel drive. Hairy and downy woodpeckers flit among the leafless trees. Their vivid coloration brightens a day misting with rain. I string up a brace of nymphs and an indicator. The easy part. It goes south from there.

I lose my first two nymphs on the initial cast and, over the next two hours, fish poorly, committing every conceivable rookie error like tying poor knots, lobbing casts into bushes, losing flies to trees on back casts, snagging my rig on unseen underwater rock. At least I don't fall in, but I come close. Then, as if in an Act of Mercy, a heavier downfall prompts a retreat to the car.

There is something to be said about sitting quietly in the Jeep and enjoying the rhythmic patter of the rain, its separate drops disintegrating into tiny jewels as they splash and set on the hood. It also prompts critical considerations. *You're a fool*, I think, *you're fishing like a rookie, losing flies like a champ and you don't care*. I say aloud, "I'm just happy to be here."

It's that simple.

When the rain subsides, I give it one more go. Not because I believe I'll catch a fish. I fish because the Whitewater spell holds me.

I quietly approach a downstream lie, sliding awkwardly down a six foot cut bank to reach a spot which offers a reasonable chance of casting upstream into a virgin riffle.

The first offering plops heavily in the current, above the holding water and the weighted nymphs drift into the feeding lane. Then the indicator mysteriously stops, a sign any attentive trouter would take as a clue to set the hook, but one perceived as a snag prompting an irritated stripping of line to clear it. Call it dumb luck that the action unwittingly pierces the upper jaw of a fourteen inch rainbow.

Uttering a few grateful words of thanks, I release the fish. It slips through my hands and disappears in the depths. How can such an intensely colored fish become so immediately invisible?

A ten inch brown takes the next cast. On the third, an eight inch brookie eats the pink Ray Charles, not the Hare's Ear the brown gulped. Three fish on three casts. A religious man might call it a Holy Trinity. I call it good fortune.

I should leave it there. Should count my blessings and walk away. But you know that doesn't happen. I sacrifice my flies to a river side tree on the very next try. Time to call it a day.

Sobered and reminded of my insubstantial place in the universe, I take the back way home along Highway 74. The North and Middle branches of the Whitewater combine in Elba. Immediately downstream, the South Fork joins the main stem and the road traces the river's course through a scenic wildlife management area. The valley widens as the Whitewater approaches its confluence with the Big River where I steer north, cruising up Highway 61 along the strikingly beautiful Mississippi toward home.

I know I'll go again before the weather turns bitter. I'll go because I might catch another beautiful rainbow. I'll go because I love trying to wrap my mind around the age of Whitewater valley rock. I'll go because I love the sound of running water. Trout fishing is merely what takes me there. Wonder keeps me there.

✳

Montana: An Ocean of Prairie

@1600 words

February 2008/Winter 2019

I'm standing in the wind, gassing an Explorer full of fly rods at a Bismarck convenience stop when a red faced, balding stranger approaches and starts talking. He requests the slightly off-color punch line to a standard Midwestern joke, "Why is it so windy in North Dakota?" and provides the answer. Without breaking verbal stride, he leans toward me conspiratorially. "You're not a religious man, are you?" He continues before I can respond. "You know what time North Dakota girls take their panties down?"

I don't.

"Mountin' time," he says.

The talkative man rails about local gas prices and how "those Montana crooks" are really taking it to you at the pumps. He'll spend as little time as possible in the next state over. He's headed for Sheridan where gas is cheaper. That said, he bids goodbye and returns to his pickup.

A short time later we cross the Missouri, headed west. The landscape enlarges significantly as it rolls, humping its back into buttes, hinting at forms of the badlands to come, stretching to a truly distant horizon. We enter the Mountain Time Zone and I finally get the man's joke.

By midafternoon we've passed the badlands and gained elevation and crossed the Yellowstone at Glendive…but let's back up. These Montana fishing trips are all Brian Brown's fault. He and his dad first took me in 1993. I've been traveling there ever since. Now it heads the list of my all-time sacred places.

◈

West Meadow Beach is also a sacred place. A rock-strewn, North Shore littoral bearing moraine from as far north as the Canadian Shield, West Meadow divides Smithtown Bay from a sinuous tidal creek which nourishes a fecund wetland. I've taken stripers out of the creek's backwater, Quahogs from the bay's navigational channel, Little Necks from beneath the sand bars, beach plums off sandy scrub growth. I've walked the low tide flats with the gulls, terns and sandpipers, especially at dusk when Long Island's driven pace seems distant as the red sun that sinks gloriously behind Connecticut and turns the Sound a pale rose with afterglow. It's the first place I ever swam in a simpler time when modest cottages lined the bulk of the mile long, west facing shore. The summer homes are razed now, the beach returned to the wild—all well and good despite the ironic twist that, in a part of the country where undeveloped shoreline is worth its weight in gold, state and county officials have yet to produce any cogent and affordable land management design. Regardless, I am no longer welcome there. I do not possess the requisite resident permit to park legally in the public lot at the northern end of the spit where Trustee Road bends sharply east and leads to the mainland. If I have a home beach, it is the West Meadow I remember as a child, a memory kept alive in my mind.

In my absence, the strong tidal current reverses direction at least twice a day, rearranging sand bars at whim. The Sound continues to wear insistently at the water's edge. Night herons and bitterns stalk the wetlands; spirits haunt quieter reaches.

I used to be a salt water guy. I searched out similar mystic locations where damp air tasted salty, brine tinged the breeze and sand and scrub and water and wind married for the benefit of the whole. I shelled Assateague shores, pulled croakers from the Hatteras surf line, tended crab traps in Pamlico Sound, camped in the Cape Lookout dunes, boogie boarded on the Cumberland Island waves, rented premium Gulf front McMansions and walked the length of the St. George Island State Park strand, explored uninhabited Gulf island beaches where wild hogs root for ghost crabs and salt water crocs leave unmistakable slitherings. There was a time when the word *vacation* inextricably attached itself to the beach.

But the sun seasoned my hide. When I swim the salt in these scientifically enlightened times, I wear a polo, collar up and buttoned at the neck, to ward off damaging solar rays and irksome sea nettles. As a youthful life guard, I slathered myself with iodine-treated baby oil to intensify the sun's rays; now I wear the strongest sun block on the market. Since dermatologists have frozen precancerous spots from my facial skin, I hide under a wide brimmed straw hat. Those precautions do not prevent me from visiting the beach but, as a transplanted Midwesterner, the cost/

distance factor is prohibitive—and please do not call sand transported to a Minnesota lakeside location by the name *beach*. I confess to snobbery on that score.

Then last summer, as a part of our annual Long Island family pilgrimage, my wife suggested we take an ocean excursion by hopping the Fire Island ferry and I caught myself employing a mental scale, weighing convenience and comfort against sunburn, uncomfortably placed sand grains and appendage shrinking north Atlantic water. At first blush, I'd describe this hesitancy as *the old fart syndrome,* but I know in a heartbeat I'd happily get burned and dirty and wade chilled rivers in the Montana outback. I am smitten by Montana and, more particularly, by its open places where clear running water provides healthy habitat for wild trout and other living things.

This shift did not occur by flipping a mental circuit breaker. Nor did it arrive through any conscious thought process. It developed at glacial pace, a kind of emotional evolution of which I remained unaware.

Not long ago I read a mystery about a female BLM officer who consorted with Pueblo *curanderas.* The author gives the officer a pet wolf christened with the Spanish name, *Montana.* It's taken me years to make the connection between the Spanish word for mountain and the name of a united state, one which has captured my imagination. In that reading moment, it came to me: once I couldn't wait to go to the beach, now I can't wait to go west.

While less creaky jointed acquaintances speak disparagingly of the drive from Saint Paul to Montana, I love the process. Friends bitch about Dakota-induced boredom. I eagerly leave Minnesota, happy at the realization the next serious sized city lies somewhere west of my intended destination. Without doubt I continue to possess a certain degree of Manhattan snobbishness which mentally reduces Minneapolis to a small town, thereby converting Bismarck or Billings to a handful of Interstate exits of interest only because I'd like someday to attend a horse auction at the Billings Livestock grounds.

When I drive out of Fargo, my blood pumps faster. Then I cross the Missouri and gain the elevation above the Breaks and my spirit shifts to a higher plane. I'm transfixed by the sheer breadth of the land, the avian surprises in the potholes, the roaming antelope, an occasional horse backed cowboy, the fact some interstate exits bear signs for no immediate destination. I love the spare, rolling flatness, the sheer emptiness, the wideness of the sky, the ribbon of a deserted two lane as it transects the Rocky Mountain uplift in eastern Montana. At Glendive, I honk at bridging the Yellowstone and begin tracking its course by monitoring the ridge line it so faithfully hugs.

The drive west is a totally enjoyable aspect of any extended fishing adventure. Give me a good book speaking out of the CD, the convenience of cruise control, an influx of caffeine softened by an occasional malt beverage, and I'm mesmerized. I'm going home. Conversely, when I cross the Yellowstone pointing east, I feel I'm leaving part of my life behind.

In truth, the jumble of mountain ranges for which Montana is named is bunched in roughly one third of the state's total area, but they are impressive though their intertwining likely confuses all but the most geographically educated. There are over sixty alpine groupings, some bearing the names of explorers or presidents or tribes or beasts, some are descriptively named and make you want to know them. How could a curious person not want to explore the Sweetgrass Hills?

Despite the ubiquity of the western peaks and their inviting remoteness, I seek more avidly what runs at their lowest levels—or Freudianly enough, what courses through the creases and hollows between them. I seek the magic of rivers and to understand more fully the web of life forms living there.

Upon reflection, while I could wax with marginally poetic words about the joys of fly fishing and of haunting the places where wild trout live, there is a common identic principle of my personal connection to open vistas. Whether it is the unknowable, mystic expanse of uninterrupted salt water or the unpopulated reach of a northern plain rolling to a distant ridge, the vastness, the wideness of creation and the whispering wind appeal to some ancient sensibility.

And thus it is that not much has changed. I still seek open space and need to wander under a wide sky where the horizon is seemingly limitless, and the ocean of prairie or water runs uninterrupted to the horizon. Perhaps then, the emotional shift I've experienced has less to do with trout than it has to do with these essentials. I can walk quietly among the dunes and pull a gorgeous striper from a Cape Cod surf line or fish at sundown in the shadow of the Tobacco Roots and hoist a muscled trout from cold, clear Missouri River water. The air might taste different, but the proportion is similar, my personal size reduced a hundredfold, and the background music is still insistent and watery.

✷

The Kinnickinnic: Home Water

@1570 words

August 2003/May 2019/Summer 2021

I've discovered sacred spots in every place I've ever lived. These treasured sections of the planet grabbed me, possessed me. I can't tell you why. West Meadow Beach flats, the Grinnell tracks, the Princeton Institute woods, Pennsylvania's King's Gap. As I moved and left those retreats behind, I don't remember consciously searching for their replacements. Maybe it's more accurate to say those locations found me. I know the Kinni did—a quiet, unassuming waterway that winds for twenty-plus miles through two counties and drains one hundred seventy-four square miles of west central Wisconsin farm and canyon land.

I keep no log of youthful fishing stories and came to fly fishing late. Gradually, imperceptibly, I began gravitating to places where trout hang out. Unremarkable at first glance, the Kinnickinnic River insinuated into my consciousness as a special personal space. Perhaps that's its special charm: so unremarkable it is remarkable. I'd like to think I know it now. I am familiar with its footpaths, know where the trout congregate and have accorded idiosyncratic names to its pools. I've seen it change too. Living things always change.

The river owns three distinct personalities and its only settlement, River Falls, does the dividing. The river's a blue map squiggle north of I-94 in Warren Township near Hawkins Cemetery where Irish immigrant families first laid their own to rest beginning in the 1850s. Originally a prairie river that coursed through largely open country, brook trout loved swimming there. Big ones. Then came the trappers, followed by the loggers. Once they cleared through, farmers burned the stumps and plowed the fields. Livestock and erosion destabilized stream banks. Some erected grist mills there. Saint Paul eateries developed a market for brook trout. You get the idea. The river changed. There are places where you'd fish. Places where you wouldn't. And the upper river is much easier to access in the spring before emerging undergrowth inhibits exploration.

A modest stream flows under the bridge at the northern outskirts of River Falls. Then the river meets a dam. There are two in town, Junction Falls and Powell Falls. They create Lake George and Lake Louise, heavily sedimented impoundments connected by a flowage that comprise the Kinni's middle section. Immediately below the second dam, the South Fork adds its volume to the flow.

Drive south through the River Falls downtown and steer into a suburban development. Turn right on River Ridge and park on the pavement among a collection of middle class homes. If there is such a thing as an oxymoronical experience, it happens each time I park there and hike downhill into the Kinni canyon. There's limited public access from this point downriver. No road parallels it. Canyon topography precludes development. If you could hike without trespassing, you'd walk approximately seven river miles before encountering the only span that crosses the lower river near its confluence with the St. Croix. The County F Bridge.

Upstream at River Falls, well-trod riverside trails quickly devolve into a narrow fisherman's path. This is the part of the river I know and like best. A separate river really. Though the area near the dam is heavily used, a willing hiker or boater can discover a good piece of solitude. Just keep going downriver. Here the Kinni expresses its true mystery and I, for one, feel a sense of wilderness and isolation. Walk far enough and walk into another reality.

Approximately two million years ago the region bore a series of glacial mantles. The ice advanced, retreated and deposited northern sands and rock and gravels in its wake—what is known as glacial drift. Meltwater carved canyons and caves, veining the area with sinks, underground springs and coulees. Larger lakes developed. At one point, a cold lake covered a significant portion of the River Falls region.

Many believe the Kinni is part of the Driftless Region, so named because the last glacial period, roughly twelve thousand years before the present, did not cover it with ice. More progressive thinkers disagree with this notion. There is evidence of glacial drift in Pierce and St. Croix counties. Geologists believe that drift was deposited in the Kinni region and it gradually eroded away. They locate the northern demarcation of the Driftless Region much farther south, below the Wisconsin River.

The Kinni canyon has slowly widened under the influence of two principal architects. Gravity continues to take its toll from above, while the basement river does its own erosional work, persistently creating its own design. It has patiently worn through a pair of *Prairie du Chien* limestone formations which are divided by a layer of sandstone.

This rock began its life as sediments deposited about four hundred and fifty to five hundred million years ago when Wisconsin's tectonic plate rested under a shallow equatorial sea. You'll find fossils if you look hard enough—snails, shellfish, corals. You can see evidence of an ancient sea floor in the form of ripple marks set in stone, striations formed by tidal flow over sand bars. Remarkable. And yes, there was salt water here. Some organic growth in the canyon is native to saline laced water.

The Kinnickinnic watershed hosts almost five hundred plant species, fully forty percent of those found Wisconsin-wide. Biologists have identified about a hundred kinds of nonvascular plants—lichens and mosses. Fifty percent of the state's bird species are found there. Warbler migrations are a source of wonder. But that's not all. Some of the flora and fauna is rare: dotted blazing star, Carolina anemone, the pallid shiner, kitten tails, the regal fritillary, snow trillium, the river redhorse, Torrey's sedge, marbleseed, *pomme-de-prairie* and round pigtoe.

There are also endangered or threatened species, pieces of original prairie, rare oak savannahs, boreal forest remnants—balsam, yellow birch, yew. There are goat prairies, sedge meadows and weeping cliffs.

The watershed has endured civilization's slings and arrows for centuries as humans failed to realize their responsibility for caring and maintaining our environment. In 1970, a UW-River Falls survey did not find trout in the lower river. Nevertheless, the region owns a pedigree of preservationist movement. Farmers, the Federal Soil Conservation Service, the Wisconsin Department of Natural Resources, Trout Unlimited and the University of Wisconsin have all chipped in to save the watershed.

The City of River Falls hasn't turned its back either. A river scene, replete with an outsized leaping brown trout, adorns a brick wall on a downtown building at the corner of North Main and West Division streets. On a more serious level, tax dollars have upgraded sewage treatment facilities, built storm water retention basins and created a dam release program. River Falls and Clifton townships have adopted resource protection ordinances. And there's a *Free the Kinni* movement afoot to remove the two dams. Though approvals to return the river to its free-flowing state are in place, I won't live to see that time.

One of the principal proponents of river conservation arrived in town in 1993. The Kinnickinnic River Land Trust is a private, non-profit organization dedicated to conserving and protecting the river environment. It cooperates with landowners, various organizations, agencies and citizens in a wholehearted effort to conserve an area increasingly threatened by urban sprawl. The Trust employs a variety of strategies to acquire and/or protect land from development. It helps property owners establish conservation easements—legal non-forfeiture agreements that permanently protect and conserve the land and water. The Trust also negotiates land purchases, donations and gifts by will in pursuit of the same end. Volunteers form the grassroots heart of the KRLT. They literally clean up the river, remove trash from watershed roadsides, dig out invasive species and restore native prairie. It is not inaccurate to say the KRLT now serves as a watershed watchdog.

The Kinnickinnic River continues to be the subject of extensive scientific scrutiny and is a model for the ways cooperative citizens and agencies can combine efforts and resources to keep a river clean. Thanks to decades of truly remarkable local, state and fed-sponsored water management, farm erosion control, bank stabilization and runoff programs, many believe the river supports the region's most notable fishery. Wild brown trout now live in the lower river. The last significant stocking occurred in 1974.

The word *Kinnickinnic* derives from Cree and Chippewa dialects. Its literal meaning translates roughly into *that which is mixed*. It describes a kind of native smoking mixture made from the inner bark of willows which is peeled into thin curls, toasted and combined with dried native tobacco or sumac before it is stuffed into pipe bowls and ignited in ceremonial smoking rituals.

The name is apt. The sum of the Kinnickinnic experience is indeed a mixture: from settlement history, to geologic features, to warbler migrations, to botanical cataloguing, to civic conservation efforts, to the sound of clear water bubbling insistently over stone older than time. When I fish there, I'm not certain if I go for the catching—or if it's to walk and wade in the aging and peaceful canyon.

It's a wonder that such a place still exists, hidden in a crevice in the earth, a literal anomaly found only thirty-odd miles from a major metropolitan area of over two million citizens. Each time I walk down the steep path to the river, the soothing melody of fresh running water typically reaches my ears before I see the stream. I've begun to think the sound is welcoming me home.

Bibliography

Cordua, William. Professor of Geology and Mineralogy, University of Wisconsin-River Falls, River Falls, WI 54022.

Erickson, Jeff. "Highway 61 Revisited-Going Driftless in Midwestern Spring Creek Country," Fish & Fly, Summer 2002.

Humphrey, J. R, "The Kinnie," Fly Fisherman, date unavailable, Kinnickinnic River Land Trust website, July 2002.

Kinnickinnic River Land Trust website. 265 Mound View Rd, Suite C, P.O. Box 87, River Falls, WI 54022.

Sincere thanks to Bill Cordua for the lesson he provided in Driftless Region geology. It was a pleasure to gain a partial glimpse into the ways a trained geologist looks at the living landscape.

✳

The Kinnickinnic: A Terrible Beauty

@1260 words

July 2021

If you're a trout person, you probably feel ownership for a favored river. You've walked it, waded it, scrambled up and down its banks, know its secret places and seasons. You know where the redstarts usually nest, when to expect the red-wings to return, where trout lilies bloom and mint patches flourish. If you're like me and wear gray hair under your hat, you know how it's changed over decades under the influence of flooding and drought and keep visions of how it used to be. Where an island your kids once frolicked on has washed away. Where you caught your first trout of the new millennium on your first cast in a run that is now solid ground that supports vegetation. Where a small creek once debouched into the river and now does so thirty yards upstream. You remember those things. Just like you remember the perfect cast to a lie in the shadow of a limestone boulder that hooked the perfect trout. Those memories stay with you and prompt you to define a river, or a piece of it, as Home Water.

I knew a river that way until COVID-19 invaded our world, an event magnified when our national government failed abjectly to respond in a timely and systematic fashion and, in fact, behaved as an ostrich. Sadly, wearing surgical masks ripened into a political issue. Everyone's world went to Hell in a Handbasket. Everything changed and, as a privileged Caucasian, I could afford to shutter it out, stay safe, live off the radar, let it pass.

Then early last summer, secondhand news arrived relative to the monstrous storm that drenched the Twins Cities Metro, which, I discovered, completely devastated parts of western Wisconsin on June 29, 2020. About forty miles east of home, ten inches of rain fell overnight in a torrent in River Falls, in the Kinnickinnic watershed; an equal amount saturated the next drainage over on the Rush. The subsequent runoff from the deluge turned quiet rivers into raging torrents. Flooding ripped massive trees from the earth, floated mobile homes off their moorings, jerked barn doors from hinges, relocated thousands of river boulders, mangled aluminum flatboats and created impenetrable tangles of flotsam. The water inundated hamlets, created road closures by washing out highway bridges and tearing away chunks of road bed. That's the least of the bad news. At least six families in the Rush drainage evacuated their homes, five people required air-lifting, stranded on their car roofs by the flooding; a seventy year-old man died after attempting to navigate a water-covered road.

As the region started recovering, I continued my own, learning to walk again after dramatically invasive surgery. Recuperation and the Pandemic kept me close to home. I could only imagine the worst. It couldn't be that bad, I reasoned. At worst, I could relearn the pieces of fishing river in the tempest's wake. Not a bad challenge.

It proved much worse than imagined. On an epic scale. When I finally limped back to the river in late August, I failed to recognize my old friend, kind of like a man who turns completely white after a significant heart event. In an instant, I knew what I thought I knew about the river no longer applied. The river was impossibly changed and reshaped, too difficult to describe in words.

I encountered an impassable fisherman's path, cluttered with uprooted timber flung over it like discarded pick-up sticks. In some places the path had disappeared, replaced by a river. One negotiable section of it remained in its familiar ten-feet-above-the-water-level location but was carpeted with sand left behind by the flooding, the walkway sufficiently layered to give the impression of walking along an ocean beach. The sand extended thirty feet inland from that raised section of river bank. Flotsam and jetsam there hung eye level in tree branches.

And yet, signs of hope did exist. Resilient tips of plant life peeked through the sand. The river continued to move. Just in different places. Though entire runs and riffles were ruined and redesigned, I tried to stay hopeful. Maybe we'd lost a yearling class of fish, but I felt confident of their return. I knew I could be patient. Then, in late October, more bad news arrived, an ironic kind of present received on my seventy-first birthday.

The Kinnickinnic flooding had threatened the structural integrity of the Powell Falls Dam, the lower of the two in River Falls, and necessitated a drawdown of Lake Louise to bare the concrete for inspection, an event that occurred over a two week period earlier in the month. In time, I consulted a memorandum, *Drone based Drawdown Analysis*, written by two guys from some obscure organization titled *inter-fluve*.

They described the project in technical lingo that made the procedure sound benign. I hope they felt embarrassed after submission. More charitably, I wondered if they weren't fly fishers and didn't understand. Whatever the case, they failed to mention the obvious.

The dam release completely destabilized the fishery. Sand flooded out from the bottom of the lake and completely covered existing cobble. According to the Kinnickinnic River Land Trust website, "an unexpected amount of sediment…negatively impacted water quality, the river's equilibrium and aquatic habitat." Not just for yards. For miles. In areas I used to fish, the water now runs clean and clear over a uniformly sandy bottom now void of vegetation. There's almost no place for a trout to hide. It's going to take a longer time than I am alive for the vicissitudes of river flow to uncover the cobble so vital to a healthy trout stream. When I tested the depth of the sand with a hiking pole, it sunk a good eighteen inches before striking the former river bottom.

When I walked along the river *sans* fly rod with my wife in early November, I could find no words to describe the devastation. Then a refrain written by William Butler Yeats sounded in my brain, a line from his poem *Easter 1916*.

(All) "Are changed, changed utterly: A terrible beauty is born."

One year after the flood I walked a portion of the lower river with a friend, hoping to find any encouraging sign of river revival. We walked on pedestrian paths now cleared for walking or tracked in new places and I felt initially encouraged until I saw the water. Once more, I thought of Yeats and his terrible phrase. Hoping against hope, I spoke with a young fisherman, clad in Patagonia waders and holding a pricey Sage rod. We spoke as fishers speak and I learned he'd made regular spring visits to the river. "It's been weeks since I caught a trout," he remarked wistfully.

Fifteen minutes later, I encountered another fisher. He'd gone "way downstream." "I caught a few," commented the older man as we spoke of the flood. "But I had to walk for them."

In truth, not a bad report.

The oft-quoted Heraclitus, who lived five hundred years before the birth of Christ, reportedly said, "No man steps into the same river twice." In this case, it is particularly apt. It is therefore, helpful to remember that this river ran in this approximate geographic location quite literally thousands of years before the ancient Greek philosopher allegedly spoke. It is also helpful to remember that when viewed through the lens of geologic time, my existence is but a flash of a firefly in an evening meadow. And, if we've taught our children well, it will come back for others to fish and enjoy.

Bibliography

Kinnickinnic River Land Trust website. 265 Mound View Rd, Ste C, P.O. Box 87, River Falls, WI 54022.

Yeats, William Butler. Easter, 1916, September 25, 1916.

✳

Final Cast

Sabbath Offerings

@1230 words

Spring & Summer 2019

The Rush River is busy this overcast June Sunday morning. The accesses are crowded with Minnesota automobiles, thereby dampening my hope for fishing quietly at the Koch access in El Paso, Wisconsin, the property truly a lovely gift to all who take nourishment from open land and running water. Especially in this age. Private property available to the public? Enlightened thinking in a time when fishing accesses are disappearing. I am grateful to users for appearing to treat the area gently, respectfully, that we think to return the gift of stewardship.

I am surprised when not one car is parked in the lot by the Katie handicapped fishing piers, its immediate surroundings neatly trimmed by the Eau Galle-Rush River Sportsman's Club. They must be good people, too, even though the majority probably voted for the Crazy Man in the White House. There is good in everyone, I suspect. A fervent hope.

I am old and injured and cannot wander rivers like I hoped I would in advanced age. The ease of access here is one of the reasons I come, and today's offering is a true gift. Though the run in front of the piers is often fished, it is available now.

The short trek to the river hurts but I ease gently into the water with the aid of a wading staff and work an olive bugger down and across the current before it slows into a deeper, quieter pool. Moving the fly with quick tugs is the ticket today. There are several glancing inquiries before a nice brown takes it in convincing fashion. A fifteen-incher could've even been sixteen since the span of my left hand takes more than two lengths to gauge it, the only measuring stick I require. A beautiful fish and a delightful Sunday offering.

Behind me I hear a succession of cars pull into the lot, rubber tires crunching and clicking over gravel. After parking, a collection of neatly dressed occupants emerges from their vehicles and mills about for no apparent reason. I wonder briefly if they've come here from church, but it is a passing thought. Eventually, they approach the river and congregate on the downstream-most fishing platform where they suspend in the corner of my eye as I continue casting. These days I tend to think more about the quality of my loops, something I wish I had started doing when I turned forty. I was too young then. I thought catching fish was important. Delusional.

A lean and tall and outdoorsy-looking silver haired man addresses the group. I hear snippets he delivers about riverine life cycles, his listeners from time to time nodding their heads in appreciation. He finishes and others speak quietly in turn, their voices drowned by river sound and bird calls.

The clouds have disappeared, and the sun is full on the water. I switch to an olive emerger out of sheer curiosity as if to ask, *Will a fish take this fly, too?* I'm having difficulty tracking the fly in the glare and sparkle on the water when another trout answers my question. My rod bends and the splashing fish attracts the bystanders' attention.

There's nothing wrong with looking like a legitimate trout fisherman, that you know what you're doing when you really don't. My vanity can use more than a little bolstering these days. Will age ever free me from this absurd male need? I unhook the fish, grip the fourteen-incher briefly with two hands and display it for all to see. They smile and clap and wave. A moment of glory.

Shortly thereafter, I notice each person taking a turn at depositing something that resembles ashes into the river. Is this a memorial service? Is this why the folks look dressed for church? I am curious, but my back is screaming a pain song only I can hear. I retreat to the bank and, out of respect for any potential memorial service, remove my hat and rest quietly on the bank. The birds are migrating through.

Bankside proceedings evidently completed, the trout-smart guy breaks away and approaches to talk fishing. I display my practiced skill of disguising a general lack of knowledge and get him talking. He's noticed tiny black stoneflies on the water. Difficult for my color-blind eyes to detect. Of course, I ask if they're conducting a memorial service.

He shrugs in conspiratorial assent. "I know it's illegal, but he was a fine fisherman and it's what he wanted."

"I hope someone does the same for me one day," I confess. An acknowledgement that I am much closer to the end than the beginning. It is a comforting thought.

"Did you know Dr. Patrick Daly?" the man queries.

I do not, so the man speaks fondly about a good fisherman, a fine doctor and a better man before trying a different tack. "Did you know Tom Helgeson?"

I did and say so. A friend, a well-known fly fisherman, conservationist, writer, publisher, editor, fly shop owner, husband and father. We shared stories over coffee from time to time. I finish with, "May Tom and Patrick rest in peace."

The man replies, "Patrick was Tom's doctor, but he couldn't keep the cancer away."

Cancer. Just about everyone has a story about it, something I learned when my son battled his and won. The man's comment prompts mine.

Years ago, Tom and I had a wide-ranging conversation over coffee after which I sent him a fishing story I'd written that somehow related to a piece of our chat. At the time Tom produced *Midwest Fly Fishing*, a newspaper-format quarterly publication. What I'd shared was not intended as a publication query, merely a gesture of friendship. Stories are a good way to share something of who you are.

Six months later, Tom published the tale and I was pleased to be referenced as a "freelance writer." Payment enough as far as I was concerned. In retrospect, I should have called Tom and thanked him. I am thanking him now and feel confident he knows I am.

Fast forward a couple of years and Tom calls for coffee and we meet in his office. He shares his battle with cancer, acknowledges he's losing, produces a check book and writes one out to me. "I owe you. I never paid you for that story."

Tom's way of squaring accounts. A poignant moment.

Trout-guy enjoys the anecdote and our communion and says so and

I'm kicking myself for not asking his name, though I did share mine. He points and singles out one person in the group. "Tom's son," he says.

"Barrett," I offer.

He nods. "Try a black stonefly. A fourteen," he suggests as he moves to rejoin the group and I rise to resume casting.

Moments later I hear the man say, "And then he wrote him a check" to which his friends respond with appreciative laughter.

The group drifts back to their cars and I am left alone on the river. I catch three more trout, eat a picnic lunch on the bench on the platform where they'd memorialized Dr. Daly. The heavier bits of his ashes rest whitely on the river bottom. Peace be with him.

Across the stream on the bank, the song thrushes are migrating through. I've never seen so many before. Certainly not so out in the open. They are beautiful.

The last of Sunday's unanticipated offerings.

N.B. Out of respect for Dr. Daly I offer a piece from his 2019 obituary in the St. Paul Pioneer Press, June 2019. Patrick? I wish I knew ye: "Dr. Patrick J. Daly, a renowned physician and passionate fly angler from Newport, died January 24, 2019. He was 87. Known for his baritone voice, thundering laugh and mischievous bushy eyebrows, Patrick had an abiding love of opera, books, fine Malbec and great meals. Born February 11, 1931, in New York City, Patrick was raised in Ireland. Patrick finished University College Dublin Medical School in 1955 and then completed medical residencies in Ireland and London. Then Patrick accepted a medical residency at the University of Minnesota Medical School. Afterward, he formed a medical practice in St. Paul. He quickly gained a reputation for his relentless devotion to patients and a pervasive distaste for hospital administrators."

If probability holds, I have another ten years left on this earth. I have composed a list of places for my wife and children to consider distributing my ashes, places I consider sacred. Because they are. I hope everyone has sacred places: West Meadow Beach, Long Island—on the sandbars at sunset. King's Gap State Park, Pennsylvania. The Princeton Institute Woods, New Jersey—at the base of the big beech tree. Yellow Breeches Creek, Pennsylvania. St. George Island State Park, Florida. The Kinnickinnic River, Wisconsin. Artist's Point,

Grand Marais, Minnesota. Crow Tribe Overlook, Ok-A-Beh Marina Road, Montana. Wind River Peak, Wyoming. The Grinnell Tracks—north out of town, look for the wild asparagus in the fencerows, though there is a golf course there now. Cape Lookout, North Carolina—in the dunes by the light house. The Van Velsor plot at St. John's cemetery, Cold Spring Harbor, Long Island. The Carr plot at Elmwood cemetery, Charlotte, North Carolina. The Boulder River at McLeod, Montana. The Whitewater River, Minnesota. The Bighorn River, Montana. The Rush River, El Paso, Wisconsin—at the Koch Property river bend among the wildflowers. The Cedar Chapel on the Brule River, Minnesota—on the path below County 45 near Grand Marais. By the Andrew Hersche headstone, the old grave yard, Hershey Mennonite Church, New Milltown, Pennsylvania. By the Robert Carr headstone, the old first grave yard, Sugaw Creek Presbyterian Church, Charlotte, North Carolina.

✶

Postscript

Stage Three
@105 words
October 2021

More than forty-three years after first stringing up a fly rod and wading into a Wind River range trout stream, it's more apt than ever to absorb *Carpe Diem* admonition as advancing decades and invasive spine surgery have dramatically reduce my strength, stamina and balance. This is something younger men do not understand.

It is now an uncomfortable chore to remain upright for extended periods of time, as if an unseen someone shadows me and keeps a vice grips locked onto my backbone, and the simple act of scaling a river bank often reduces me to sliding or crawling, depending on direction of travel. And yet, I am too young to not to put the next foot forward, albeit slowly and deliberately.

The other day I fished roughly one third of the length of Pine Creek that I intended to cover as the bushwhacking to navigate its edges proved laborious and the overgrown meadowed area offered no fallen trees or boulders to rest on or against. I retired to the car a little more than an hour after starting, unfolded a lawn chair, basked in the sun, savored a picnic lunch, a cold Wisconsin beer and the taste of fall in the air. It fell to me to determine my reaction toward the foreshortened fishing experience. I could express frustration, discouragement, even anger. Or savor the moment. Alone in a bucolic creek valley in the silence and brightness of an autumn day.

The decision remains mine. And I am determined to be present, to taste and smell and feel and hear the moments I have left on rivers. And to be grateful for what's given. To know that the simple act of a brown trout appearing, seemingly out of nowhere, in one electric instant, under my proffered grasshopper fly and subsequently putting a pleasing bend into my fly rod is an event as rewarding as the first time I experienced it over forty years ago.

In my fishing life I have reached Sophocles' Third Stage of Man and now walk tentatively on three legs, a wading staff affixed to my belt by a retractable cord. Though I've fished over two dozen times this past season, I'm aware each time I step away from the river, I might have taken my last cast and that thought is unsettling. Especially since I might then have to learn to play golf. So I approach the fishing time I have left thoughtfully and challenge myself to savor each moment—the comforts and discomforts. To give thanks to the earth, the sky, the water. To take away a cherished moment from each trip, such as an overhead visual of a beaver swimming upstream, under water in a clear running creek. I want store these moments while I continue to put the next foot forward until I absolutely cannot.

 End

Printed in the USA
Publisher's number

Printed in the United States
by Baker & Taylor Publisher Services